'It's impossible to overestimate how completely Phillip Lopate's anthology *The Art of the Personal Essay* reframed and revivified the personal essay for contemporary American writers and readers. In his new collection of essays, *Portrait Inside My Head*, Lopate demonstrates his own immense virtues as an essayist – his ceaseless ability to "think against" himself.' – David Shields

'What holds it together is an engaging voice, the projection of a curious, appealingly modest, sometimes self-mocking character behind that voice, and "the fluent play of a single consciousness." He's gifted at staging his inner conflicts, radiating intimacy without descending into the confessional.' – *The New York Times Book Review*

'Hilarious and tender . . . Meandering merrily along in the footsteps of the great classical essayists Montaigne and William Hazlitt, acclaimed cultural critic Lopate traipses breezily through family life and literary, cultural, social, and political matters . . . with his typical elegance and peripatetic curiosity.' – *Publishers Weekly*

Phillip Lopate is an essayist, novelist and poet. He is the author of more than a dozen books, including three personal essay collections – *Bachelorhood*, *Against Joie de Vivre* and *Portrait of My Body*; a critical study, *Notes on Sontag*; and *To Show and to Tell: The Craft of Literary Nonfiction*. He directs the graduate nonfiction program at Columbia University and lives in Brooklyn with his wife and daughter.

Phillip Lopate

–

# PORTRAIT INSIDE MY HEAD

Notting Hill Editions

Published in 2015
by Notting Hill Editions Ltd
Widworthy Barton Honiton Devon EX14 9JS

Designed by FLOK Design, Berlin, Germany
Typeset by CB editions, London

Printed and bound
by TJ International, Padstow, Cornwall



A CIP record for this book
is available from the British Library

ISBN 978-1-907-90396-0

www.nottinghilleditions.com

# *Contents*

Introduction

# – In Defense of the Miscellaneous Essay Collection –

Reader, you have in your hands a motley collection of essays, personal and critical.

The advantage of the heterogeneous essay collection by a single author is that it shows you how a particular mind moves through the world. If you are attracted to an essayist's mentality and way of speaking, ideally you can surrender happily to his or her take on various subject matters, the more diverse the better. Let us see how our author will tackle this particular memory, neurotic tic, political or social problem, book, movie, play, comic strip, rock band, without requiring an over-arching theme.

If there is a consistent theme in this particular collection, it is the discovery of limitations, and learning to live with them. The recognition of one's limits, painful as it may be, can have salutary side-effects. In my case, it absolves me of the need to be both a hero and a coward, an explorer and a stay-at-home, a saint and a villain, a loyal husband and a Don Juan, a political activist and a skeptic, a spiritual mystic and a rationalist atheist, a performing athlete and a sports fan, a great if excruciatingly self-demanding literary stylist and a prolific if merely good-enough writer. Granted, we are all comprised of numerous shards, and incorporate many contradictory selves in our make-up. But over the course of time we choose, or the choice is made for us by fate, circumstance, whatever name you care to give it. The acknowledgement that one is tied to a fairly predictable set of behaviors and responses, and is not an amorphous blob of open receptivity, can certainly be a source of strength, even as it implies some rigidity. I concede that we probably use only a small portion of our human potential. Americans are accustomed to think that a person has almost unlimited capacity for growth. *Anything is possible; if you want it enough, go for your dream.* While it may be un-American to say so, just speaking for myself I have learned over the course of a lifetime that I am quite limited, and I find that knowledge reassuring. Though I continue to learn new things and accept new challenges, I am no longer in the process of becoming: I may be an unfinished man but I am more or less *a closed book*. What better way to show that finality than in a collection largely of personal essays? For the personal essay is uniquely suited to expose this continuous bumping up against limits, against the borders of the self – which is one good reason I cling to it.

At the same time, I consider the essay to be a wonderfully fluid form, possessing the freedom to wander in search of sudden discovery. It has a long, glorious history as a literary testing-ground of intellectual thought and psychological self-portraiture; and a heterogeneous assemblage of essays offers an ideal field in which to demonstrate the form's range. The risk is to be told that 'Collections of multi-purpose, previously published prose are often bitty and unsatisfying,' as one *TLS* reviewer phrased it. Yet I persist in putting forth a collection that will include my musings on childhood, movies, literature, friendship, marriage, parenthood, sex, and the nail parings of daily life, so that the reader can enjoy the fluent play of a single consciousness, a sensibility flowing through disparate subject matters. I persist because I know the truth, which is that, deep down, you love essays. You may be ashamed to admit it. But you love essays, you love essays, you are getting very sleepy, you *lo-o-ove* essays . . .

An essay collection is a distinctly different adventure from a memoir. A fiercely accomplished essayist I know was advised to dismantle her collection of personal essays and restructure it as a memoir. She spent a year trying to do so, only to decide in the end that it wouldn't work, that the original form had its integrity that it made no sense to camouflage. Emily Fox Gordon, in 'The Book of Days', put her finger on one difference between the two genres when she argued that the memoir seems to have a built-in redemptive bent by the very nature of the author's having survived to tell the tale, the how-I-got-over aspect. In her words,

> the memoir and the personal essay are crucially different forms. The memoir tempts the memoirist to grandiose self-representation. The essay, with its essential modesty, discourages the

impulse . . . The erratic zigzag of essayistic thinking – what has been called thinking against oneself – makes the essay proof against the triumphalism of memoir by slowing the gathering of narrative momentum. The essayist *transects* the past, slicing through it first from one angle, then from another, until – though it can never be captured – some fugitive truth has been definitively cornered.

When I was editing my anthology *The Art of the Personal Essay*, I was uncomfortably aware that I might be drawing an overly pronounced distinction between personal and formal essays, by including just those examples from my authors that were most personal. William Hazlitt was a well-known drama and art critic as well as one of the most relentlessly self-scrutinizing essayists; George Orwell wrote about Henry Miller, Mohandas Gandhi and Charles Dickens, not just about his school days; James Baldwin's first collections included pieces about 'Everyone's Protest Novel' and the movie *Carmen Jones* along with his signature autobiographical essay, 'Notes of a Native Son'; and Virginia Woolf wrote hundreds of pages of exemplary literary criticism and reflections on current affairs. It was not that these writers compartmentalized their personal and analytical essay sides: everything that interested them carried a personal water-mark, just as every attempt to understand their experiences was inflected with the detached analytical intelligence they employed as critics. The books we read, the movies we see, the public spaces we inhabit, the historical cataclysms and bizarre tabloid scandals that preoccupy us are as much a part of our autobiographies as the familial struggles, substance-abuse problems, or other illnesses that test our psyches.

As recently as the 1950s and 1960s, it was understood that an essay collection like *On the Contrary* by Mary McCarthy would and should include her musings on the Broadway play season, Gandhi, the Kinsey Report on American sexual behavior, and Simone de Beauvoir, along with some amazing memoir-pieces such as 'My Confession' and 'Settling the Colonel's Hash', while Leslie Fiedler's miscellany *An End of Innocence: Essays on Culture and Politics* would range in lively fashion from Alger Hiss, Senator McCarthy and the Rosenbergs to *Roman Holiday, Huckleberry Finn*, F. Scott Fitzgerald and a travel journal through Italy. The motley character of these assortments was part of their allure. I don't see why those pleasures should be only a thing of the past, any more than poetry or short story collections would be considered passé.

Is my polemic beginning to sound transparently self-serving? I am only advocating the pleasures of the genre in which I toil and the unsung delights of the miscellaneous single-author essay collection, not arguing for my place in the essay pantheon. I am no Hazlitt by any stretch of the imagination. Still, I take heart from what my hero once wrote, after watching some Indian jugglers tossing up four brass balls:

I ask what there is that I can do as well as this? Nothing. What have I been doing all my life? Have I been idle, or have I nothing to show for all my labor and pains? Or have I passed my time in pouring words like water into empty sieves, rolling a stone up a hill and then down again, trying to prove an argument in the teeth of facts, and looking for causes in the dark and not finding them? Is there no one thing in which I can challenge competition, that I can bring as an instance of exact perfection, in which others cannot find a flaw? The utmost I can pretend for is to write a description of what this fellow can do. I can write a book: so can many others who have not even learned to spell. What abortions are these Essays! What errors, what ill-pieced transitions, what crooked reasons, what lame conclusions! How little is made out and that little how ill! Yet they are the best I can do. I endeavor to recollect all I have ever observed or thought upon a subject, and to express it as nearly as I can. Instead of writing on four subjects at a time, it is as much as I can manage to keep the thread of one discourse clear and unentangled. I have also time on my hands to correct my opinions, and polish my periods; but the one I cannot, and the other I will not do.

That *Hazlitt* could have thought so poorly of his efforts! But what really sticks in my mind is his last statement: he will not polish and perfect his essays. Is it because he is obstinate and lazy, or because the nature of the essay form is such that – unlike the poem and the short story – it does not readily permit of crystalline perfection. It is too open to the incidental, too impure, too forgiving. Maybe that's why I love it so much. I am not a perfectionist, neither by temperament nor prose style. I am drawn to the shagginess of the essay, its discontinuous forms of consciousness, and for much the same reason, to the unavoidable yet unapologetic unevenness of the miscellaneous essay collection.

It was Charles Lamb, that other great English essayist, who warned of the dangers and the requirements involved in such an enterprise, in a review of his friend Hazlitt's *Table Talk*: 'A series of Miscellaneous Essays, however well-executed in the parts, if it have not some pervading character to give a unity to it, is ordinarily as tormenting to get through as a set of aphorisms, or a jest-book.' Lamb cited Plutarch, Montaigne, Samuel Johnson and Hazlitt as those who were able to get away with it: that is, impart a pervading character or unity to an essay collection's heterogeneous parts. The bar had been raised very high indeed. Let us lower it a little, for pity's sake and my own.

# – Tea at the Plaza –

What is important to an adult and what matters to a child are so often at variance that it is a wonder the two ever find themselves on the same page. Parents may feel an occasional urge to spend money extravagantly on their offspring, only to discover that it means very little to the children themselves. You buy an expensive antique Raggedy Ann doll for your kid that she tosses in a corner, thinking it ugly and musty, meanwhile being enthralled by the shiny plastic action figure they give out free at McDonald's. And yet, if you're like me, you keep falling into the trap of costly, unappreciated presents, perhaps because they're not really for your child but for the child-self in you who never got them when you were growing up.

I remember, when my daughter, Lily, was four, my wife, Cheryl, and I sprang for a family carriage ride through Central Park in the snow. We had such an idyllic Currier & Ives image in our heads, and it seemed such an ideal treat for the holidays – all the more special because we were dyed-in-the-wool New Yorkers and usually stayed clear of what the tourists went in for. 'Let's just do it!' we cried impulsively, determined to play at being tourists in our own city. Yet

I could not help noticing the reluctant, even alarmed expression on Lily's face as she climbed, or was lifted, into the barouche, behind the bewhiskered coachman with the tall shamrock hat, stationed across from the Plaza Hotel. We started off at a slow trot; the carriage entered the park, my wife and I entranced by the vista, and Lily beginning to whimper and complain that she was cold, until she spotted a merry-go-round, the prospect of which excited her far more than an actual horse giving her a ride. As we neared the merry-go-round, Lily became so insistent that we had to ask the coachman to stop the carriage. I forked over what felt at the time like major dough for a fifteen-minute trot, grumbling as she ran to the carousel.

I vowed under my breath that I would never be such a patsy again. But we had not yet gotten out of the business, my wife and I, of manufacturing exorbitant 'perfect memories' for our daughter to cherish all her days. So we took her to Broadway shows, and to the *Nutcracker* ballet (where she fell asleep), and we began – at first vaguely, then with more urgency – plotting an afternoon's high tea at the Plaza's Palm Court. Somehow that corner at Fifty-Ninth Street and Fifth Avenue was the Bermuda Triangle that kept sucking us into fantasies of civilized luxury. You must understand that this was not a case of passing on some proud family tradition: my father took me not to Brooks Brothers for a fitting of my first suit but to the back room of a Gypsy shop that probably trafficked in stolen goods.

I grew up in working-class Brooklyn, and never entered the Plaza when I was a child, nor did Cheryl, who hailed from hardscrabble upstate New York and might, if she were lucky, get to order a hot chocolate with whipped cream at the local luncheonette. But our child was a middle-class New York child, thanks to our fatiguing efforts to claw our way up the social ladder, and, by God, we were bound and determined to give her all the social graces and sophisticated experiences that befit her, if not our, station in life.

So, with somewhat grim if hearty countenances, we got Lily and ourselves all dressed up, and took her into Manhattan for the thrill of a lifetime. We did not ride the subway from Brooklyn, mind you, as that would have spoiled the general effect, but drove in and, unable to find a parking spot on the street, left our car in a garage a few blocks east of the Plaza, in what must be the most expensive parking area in the planet. But hey! Who cares about the expense? We're treating ourselves! We entered the regal steps of the Plaza, which had on powerful electric warmers, and stood in line at the perimeter of the majestic Palm Court.

I had already called ahead and knew they did not take reservations over the phone; but fortunately the 4.00 p.m., midafternoon line was not that long, and we were assured of seating. In fact, business seemed relatively slow, for a treasured landmark. We oohed and aahed at the fabulous high ceiling, the palm trees, the piano, the marble floor, and the fashionably or laughably costumed Ladies Who Lunched. Lily nodded, smiling and looking dutifully about, but seemed a bit cool toward it all, as if she were indulging her parents' naïve enthusiasm. Once seated, we took up our menus stiffly. The waitress wrote down our orders – three specials with all the trimmings, O spare not the clotted cream, the crème fraîche, the clabber, or what have you, the peach cobblers, the jams, the crustless cucumber sandwiches, the savories, the petits fours, the works! All that centuries of human ingenuity had found to include in this cozy English tradition of High Tea, we wanted. 'Think of it, Lily, Eloise herself ran through this very same room!' I said.

'But she's not real, is she?' said my knowing six-year-old.

'No, but still –'

'Of course she is!' insisted my wife, ever eager to prolong childhood credulity, be it about Santa Claus, the Tooth Fairy, or Eloise. She darted me a scolding look, warning me away from shortening our daughter's childhood with my 'realism'.

So we kept it Nice; we were all on our best behavior, and commented favorably, when the food came, on the beautiful tea service, the exquisite arrangement of edibles, the deliciousness of everything – in short, it was a dull conversation, but appropriately so, duly dull. We were proud of ourselves for adhering to the parts assigned us in this civilized ritual, for coloring within the lines. No one would ever guess we lived in Brooklyn. We had stuffed ourselves, and now Lily began getting restless, as children will in that postprandial moment. Enough with the talk, she wanted action. I commiserated with her squirminess – more to the point, I felt childishly restless myself, and so I volunteered to take her for a walk about the floor. 'Should I come, too?' asked Cheryl.

'No, stay and enjoy the last of your tea.' (I was already deep in the throes of performing a Good Deed.)

It was fun to walk around with Lily and stick our noses into every corner of the nearby bar, the cloakroom, and the lobby. We pretended to be spies; she picked a person to trail after, then darted away madly in the opposite direction and hid, giggling. In our last go-round we came upon a family – a mother and her three young daughters in dresses, the youngest of whom was holding a clutch of balloons. Probably she was celebrating her birthday. Lily was instantly enchanted – not by the birthday girl, by the balloons. They were plump, filled with helium, and had marbleized patterns outside and little silver jingling bells inside. How she wanted one of those balloons! I could tell it meant everything to her at that moment; so I went over to the mother and asked her if my daughter might have one. The word *borrow* would have been dishonest, as we had no intentions of ever returning it. No, have it for free, just like that, is what I meant; it was a brazen request to make of a perfect stranger, and fortunately the kind woman understood what was at stake and acquiesced. 'Which one would you like?' she asked Lily. Stalled between the pink, the blue, and the red, Lily finally chose the red. The woman then turned to her daughter and asked ceremoniously, 'Would you mind giving this little girl one of your balloons?' The girl, obviously a well-brought-up child, gravely assented, and Lily walked away holding its string, happy – in ecstasies – as happy as I'd ever seen her.

We were both pretty high, delighted with our luck, when we sat back at the table. There is something marvelous in a place like the Plaza about getting something for free, even if it's just a twenty-five-cent balloon. My wife wanted to know the whole story, and Lily began telling it, with her usual dramatic flair and embellishments. As she was gesticulating to make a point, she lost hold of the end of the string and the balloon floated up to the ceiling. How many seconds it took to make its ascent, I could not begin to tell you, but the subjective experience was one of quite extensible duration: just as in a car crash your whole life, they say, flashes through your mind, or just as a glass rolling off the table takes forever when you can do nothing to arrest its fall, so my accumulated past of error, catastrophe, and missed opportunity fluttered before my eyes while I watched the balloon drift up, up, languidly taking its time. Was I passing on my destiny of disenchantment and lost illusions to my daughter? It was too horrible to contemplate. What is even more unconscionable is that a part of me wanted to laugh.

This despicable urge to laugh arose in me, in spite of (or maybe because of . . .) the fact that Lily had started wailing. Piercing sobs issued from her as she watched her balloon (which had only been hers for five minutes) escaping further and further. The diners at nearby tables stopped midfork, perhaps readying themselves to intervene in the event they saw evidence of child abuse; when they satisfied themselves that there was none, they returned to their food, most likely blaming us for not being able to control our brat better. Meanwhile the captain of the waiters hurried over to see if there was anything he could do. Our waitress began making commiserating faces and noises such as one directs at a little baby. All to no avail. My wife took Lily in her lap and started calming her down.

I attended to the check, handing over my credit card and totaling up the tip, the full amount coming to two hundred dollars. I could not rid myself of feeling chagrined that that outlay, plus the garage bill, had been nullified by the loss of a little nothing balloon. 'We'll get you another balloon as soon as we leave the hotel,' Cheryl promised Lily, who was beginning to decelerate from wrenching sobs to puppy whimpers.

After I had gotten my credit card back and we'd put our coats on and were about to leave, I turned to the simpatico wait-captain and asked him how long it would take for that balloon to come down, thinking it might be possible to retrieve it and give the story of our outing a happy ending.

'Oh, about a week, I'd imagine,' he said with a slight accent (Egyptian? Maltese?).

'And is there no way to get it down before then?'

'No way.'

For some reason, this report that it would take a week to come down set Lily off on a fresh burst of wailing. Now she was inconsolable. She was like Hecuba, experiencing precociously the fullness of grief. We hastened her out of there, but she kept up loud sobbing in the street.

'Knock it off!' said Cheryl, suddenly out of patience. 'You're making a spectacle of yourself, you're acting like a two-year-old!' While I completely agreed with my wife, I also, in that instantaneous switch of good cop–bad cop roles for which parents are so adept, became entirely sympathetic to Lily's woe: I knew that emotions do not have to be reasonable to shatter us, and that sobs feed uncontrollably on sobs, regardless of our efforts to stop them,

'Let her cry,' I said. 'I'm not embarrassed. Who cares what these people think?'

The truth was, I was strangely happy. The whole incident had struck me as funny, a cosmic comeuppance for our pretensions to being the sorts of swells who had tea at the Plaza, though it may also have been a defensive reflex arising from my powerlessness in the face of Lily's anguish. Meanwhile, Lily, as if picking up on my undertone, began to giggle, in between her sobs – a part of her perhaps recognizing that she was being ridiculous, a drama queen, making entirely too much of this. I think, though, that my errant satisfaction issued from a darker source: I felt myself bonding with my daughter in our now-shared discovery that life was composed, at bottom, of loss, futility, and ineluctable sorrow. There was nothing you could do about it but laugh.

Years later, that is precisely what we do do: whenever we recall the lost balloon, it is always good for a chuckle, and Lily, now a teenager, is the first to laugh at herself. But we know better than to return to the Palm Court for tea. In fact, speaking of loss, that elegant ballroom, which conjures up Edith Wharton's and F. Scott Fitzgerald's New York, and which we all thought would last forever, regardless of how slow business might be, is hanging by a thread. The new owners of the Plaza have turned a good part of the hotel into condominiums, and have wanted to gut the Oak Room and the Palm Court as well, but the landmarks preservation community has prevented them, for the time being. If someday these cherished interiors are demolished, as seems likely, I will be sad but I will not only be sad. The Palm Court will have gone the way of Rumpelmayer's, the legendary pink-ensconced ice cream parlor that once stood a block away from the Plaza – both institutions no longer around to torment parents with the chimera of a perfect children's outing.

# – The Camera Shop –

Whenever I see the flags, bunting, and triangular pennants announcing a store's Grand Opening, my heart does a flip-flop at this poignant fusion of patriotism and retail, as though we were all being asked as good citizens to prop up the gross national product. I cross the street to examine the window, and stare at the proprietors with their nervous, eager air. Rarely do I go into a store on its Opening Day, however: partly because I consider myself unlucky and would not want to visit my bad financial karma on a maiden establishment, but more likely because I cannot shake the *triste* memory of my parents' camera shop.

My mother, who was given to daydreams of fortune, and impatient with her dead-end clerical job in Midtown Manhattan's garment center, had hit on the idea of starting a store in Brooklyn that would sell Brownie cameras and Kodak film, take in negatives to be processed elsewhere, and act as a booking agent for Kewpie Studios, the unfortunately named enterprise of a photographer-friend of hers, Alan K., who specialized in baby and child portraits.

Now it must be said that my mother knew nothing about the technical side of photography, but she could read a Kodak box and regarded herself as a 'people person', ever ready to deal with the public. She had some retail experience, first having worked in a beauty parlor as a teenager, then having run a candy store in her twenties with my father when they were starting out as a couple. They had both remembered this candy store as one of the few happy times in their marriage: my extroverted mother had enjoyed playing confidante to the neighborhood youths, and my reserved father, while by no stretch of the imagination a people person, had gamely mixed malteds. It was agreed now that he would keep his regular job, helping my mother on weekends in the camera store.

At the time we lived in semi-squalor, barely squeaking by; my parents had virtually no capital to invest in a business, and certainly no cushion to tide them over the rough early stages of enterprise. But my energetic mother found a vacant store with low rent not too far from where we lived. In those days, when you walked up Lee Avenue a mile or so away from the center of Williamsburg, you would cross the Hasidic Jewish part to a largely African-American and Hispanic area around Myrtle Avenue, then a desperate slum. Myrtle Avenue, a gloomy street darkened by elevated trains adjacent to housing projects, had seemed to my childish imagination the furthest demarcation line, beyond which sea serpents lurked. Now we were suddenly about to operate a store on the 'wrong' side of Myrtle Avenue.

I remember Opening Day, with its flags and streamers, a pleasant Saturday in June. I was eleven. My mother sent me outside as a shill to mingle with window-shoppers and drum up business. A dozen curious spectators were craning their necks and looking in, but none seemed eager to enter the shop. Some of the remarks I overheard had a skeptical tone: 'Don't look like they got much in there.' 'They're never gonna make it.' I suddenly saw our camera shop not through my mother's hopeful eyes but through a more detached, disloyal perspective: the pathetic, meager stock of Brownie cameras and other cheap models, the nondescript fluorescent lighting, the display counters lined with brown contact paper of the sort used on kitchen pantry shelves, the spare, undecorated space, the lack of furniture save for two kitchen chairs with cheap plastic backing – all gave out the impression of someone's shabby home rather than a retail establishment. The store lacked *store*ness.

(Decades later, I would encounter this same becalmed, not-quite-retail atmosphere in East Berlin shops before the Wall came down: shops that had been so long removed from a capitalist mercantile culture that they had grown disdainful of or no longer able to project a vending aura.)

Fortunately, the camera shop managed to draw some regulars, mostly doting Puerto Rican fathers, in its opening week. I remember one particular exuberant father with an upswept pompadour, a tattoo on his arm, a cigarette pack tucked into his rolled-up T-shirt sleeve, who could not resist taking roll upon roll of his daughters in their pink Sunday dresses. It was the first time I became conscious of that passionate paternal pride that Latino men sometimes take in their offspring, and it made me envious.

'Poor people like to take pictures of their children,' my mother explained. While the maxim held true, its downside was equally true: poor people cannot always afford to pick up the printed rolls they have left for developing.

My older brother, Leonard, and I, who had been hanging around the store too much during summer vacation, were sent by our mother into the neighboring streets to collect payment. More than once I found myself in the nearby massive public housing project, all of whose brick buildings looked confusingly alike. I would ring the doorbell of the address on the yellow film envelope and, when no one answered, call out the customer's name. Sometimes I heard scurrying sounds inside, and the voices of black or Hispanic children probably no older than myself whispering, 'It's the landlord!' or 'It's the Man – don't open it!' So great was their fear of authority – welfare caseworkers, bill collectors – that even a trembling eleven-year-old like myself was accorded the power to frighten.

I had thought we were poor, but now I was seeing a level of poverty that shocked me. Meanwhile, every time my mother turned her back to keep an eye on her four children, since she could not afford babysitters, some neighborhood kid would run in and steal a camera. Thefts, deadbeat customers, and insufficient volume all doomed the business. Within six months of opening, the camera shop was closed.

My mother continued to operate Kewpie Studios from our apartment, making cold calls to strangers in the phone book. Ashamed, we would wince at her saccharine (to our ears) 'pitching' voice and mimic it behind her back. Of course she was putting on this phony voice to keep us, the family, solvent, but at the time we were purely ungrateful. Her photographer-partner, Alan K., a touchy, blade-thin guy with a wife and two bratty kids, whom I sometimes babysat for, would go out on shoots set up by my mother. Alan K. intrigued me because he had written an autobiographical novel called *The Keys to the Cage* about his sad childhood, whose traumatic secrets had been unlocked with the aid of hypnosis and Freudian analysis. Unable to find a publisher, he had paid a vanity press to print it. I am one of the few to have read this precursor of Victim Literature. He was not much of a writer (the recorded dreams were especially boring), but he took decent pictures of children, and could reasonably document a wedding, confirmation, or bar mitzvah. Eventually he and my mother quarreled, and she gave up her last connection with photography, going back to work as a clerk in the garment industry – at the time New York's largest, most dependable and forgiving employer. So ended one of those Ralph Kramdenesque schemes and pipe dreams to which my parents periodically fell susceptible, like other members of the striving working class who sought to pull themselves up by their bootstraps into the lower-middle-class Eden of proprietorship.

Recently I walked around the area where the camera shop had failed. I was surprised to find Myrtle Avenue not nearly as bleak as I remembered. Gone was the gloomy El train (torn down in 1969). The projects were still charmless and monolithic as ever. But the entire block on which the camera shop had stood was now an empty lot, tall weeds surrounded by a chain-link fence. I saw what the problem had been: location, location, location.

## – The Countess's Tutor –

Recently I brought a friend to see the old block in Fort Greene, Brooklyn, where I lived from age eleven through high school, in the mid-1950s. Parts of the neighborhood were as funky as I remembered: its bars and fortune-tellers, processed-hair parlors, fried chicken joints, and street-corner winos unchanged. Imagine my chagrin, however, when, prepared to show off the 'mean streets' of my youth, I found the crummy six-story apartment building of my early adolescence converted into condominiums, with a concierge, no less, at a lobby desk. The last time I'd bothered to check, twenty-five years before, that double-winged apartment house on Washington Avenue had looked abandoned: windows boarded up with plywood, yellow brick façades blackened like singed eyebrows by a suspicious fire. I had half-expected to see it torn down, but no, this time it was clean and gleaming, its stone-carved gargoyles displayed to perfection. I asked the concierge for permission to take the elevator to the top floor, where my family, all six of us, had lived miserably crammed together. He said yes, provided we did not disturb the present occupants. I assured him my friend and I had absolutely no desire to peer inside:

just seeing the door would suffice. We rode the elevator in silence, I noting with satisfaction its dingy brown paint job. But I was in shock when I faced the old door: 6A had been changed to PH1. Had I known then that I was living in a future penthouse, how different my sense of destiny and entitlement might have been.

Something is wrong when the slum dwellings of our youth have become the prewar desiderata of the next generation. Then again, maybe the apartment building had been initially intended as discreet, middle-class luxe, and had only gone into decline mid-twentieth century, the period during which my family lived in it, and was now restored to its original economic niche.

But that was not what I was thinking about. I was remembering the last time we had been inside that door, when my mother sprayed the kitchen for cockroaches in one final skirmish before moving out. We had fought the roaches so many years, unavailingly, but at the penultimate moment of our tenancy we got hold of a powerful DDT spray gun and cleared the food out of the kitchen. At first there were only a few. Then like a locust storm the roaches began pouring out of the stove, from behind the refrigerator, across and down the ceiling. They were dropping at our feet, doped and spinning, and we smashed them under our shoes like raisins, two at a time. It was a regular killing field: wherever we stepped, we slaughtered.

Then I gazed at the staircase, and remembered the time I descended, with heavy heart of brother-responsibility, to defend my younger sister Joan, who said she had been robbed by two black boys. I walked her around for blocks, asking her every time we approached a knot of boys, 'Are those the ones?' – as if I ever could have wrested anything from them but a beating. (Years later she confessed that no one had robbed her; she had spent the money on ice cream.)

We had moved there in the mid-1950s ostensibly because our family of six needed more room. But you don't move four growing white kids into a black slum just for the extra space. The flight from our previous Jewish neighborhood, Williamsburg (itself a run-down ghetto then), had all the stigma of exile. My parents had gotten in trouble with our last landlady and had been kicked out, simple as that. One afternoon, the landlady (who lived beneath us: always a mistake) burst into our apartment while both our parents were away at their jobs. She had two policemen with her. We kids had been running around half-naked – playing strip poker, as my brother and I liked to do with our younger sisters – but as soon as we saw the landlady and the cops enter we hid under our beds. 'You see what I mean?' she kept saying, sweeping her arms in all directions. 'It's a madhouse, a pigsty! There's no supervision, the kids run wild, it looks like it hasn't been cleaned in months. I just want you to be witnesses.' I poked my head out, but they ignored me, taking flash photographs of the disarray. I began to see my family's peculiarities from an outsider's perspective. Still, what had we done? We had let the apartment get messy – by no means criminal neglect, or even destruction of property. In a less house-proud setting, no one would have thought to complain.

When the invaders left, we came out of our hiding places and roared with laughter. Partly, it was shock, but beyond that, we were genuinely convulsed, mimicking the outrage on the landlady's face, her uptight prissiness, and the cops' picture-taking gestures. My parents, though, did not find the incident funny at all. They had to take a day off from work to answer Mrs Jacobs's charges in court. The upshot was that we were given three months to move.

So I could never get out of my mind the notion that we were living in a black section of Brooklyn as punishment – evicted from the 'Eden' of Williamsburg for being slobs. My mother remained an indifferent housekeeper, after coming home tired from her clerical job, and we kids continued to run free and not bother to clean up either. But in Fort Greene, nobody seemed to care: we could mess up the place as much as we wanted. The result was that the kitchen table acquired an intriguing fecundity of detail.

The focus of our family life was the kitchen table. Hardly a revelation: I have often read accounts of ghetto upbringings, Hispanic, African-American, Jewish, Italian, which boasted of the kitchen as the warm domestic center, dispensing nourishment, conversation, and a sense of community. However, in our case the kitchen table had something sinister and pathological about it, due to the inconceivable density of objects on its surface. Originally it had been used as a pantry annex, to catch the surplus from cupboards, but what had started in one corner of the table spread to another, so that pretty soon nothing was put away except perishables. Everything else was left on the table, where we could 'get at it easily': jelly jars, Ritz crackers, dirty dishes, matzo boxes, playing cards, coffeepot, crayons, schoolbooks, radio, tax records and insurance papers (which got spots of jam on them), mucilage, twine, sewing machine, vitamin bottles, seltzer canisters, U-Bet chocolate syrup, classical record albums from the Masterpiece of the Month club, and whatever else had wandered into our lives at the moment.

There is no question that the table's chaotic clutter expressed something about our family's character, but what, you might be asking, other than our being slobs? It was our Noah's ark, our survival raft, our environmental artwork; an overcompensation for our being poor, a visual refutation of material deprivation. The table also called attention to my mother's struggle against overweight: because she was unhappy with her marriage and her job and herself, she went on eating binges, absentmindedly downing whatever was left around, a whole box of chocolate-covered marshmallows at a time. But it was not only my mother who 'rounded out' a meal, or assuaged preprandial hungers, with snacks that took no preparation: the whole family was addicted to noshing in a dreamy, unconscious way. My father would pop one Fig Newton after another in his mouth, staring off into space, while remaining thin as Kafka's hunger artist – which naturally enraged his corpulent wife. Father's pensive passivity, his geological resistance to housework, played its part in this assemblage. But if you asked our parents how the table came to be so messy, they would have a simple answer: the children. It was the children who never cleaned up after themselves, who expected their mother to do everything like a slave, who brought whatever homework or game they were working on to the table, for the purpose of finding company there.

In truth, we did use the table as our school desk. And even I, who had the family reputation for being a neatnik, because I tried to keep a section of the bedroom I shared with my older brother, Lenny, free from clutter, would no more have thought of cleaning off the table by myself than of pruning all the trees in Brooklyn. Still, we were ashamed of the mess, and whenever anyone came over to the house, which was rare, we apologized about the table immediately. Less and less did we invite any classmates over, fearing they would not understand. My parents, on their side, seemed too fatigued by work to bother with friendships. They withdrew into themselves and gave free rein to their mania for disappointment.

—

*Well I know I got religion – certainly*
*I know I got religion – certainly, Lord*
*Well I know I got religion – certainly*
*Certainly, certainly, Lo-oord!*

Sunday mornings we would awake to the ebullient, hand-clapping sounds of gospel music from the clapboard tabernacle down the block. We would open the window and hear a free concert of 'Mary, Don't You Weep', 'Great Day in the Morning', or 'I Got a Mother over Yonder' (which we would sing sarcastically to our mother just to irritate her). That modest-looking church used to attract renowned groups on tour. My brother, Lenny, who was fast becoming a gospel and jazz aficionado, would say, 'Ohmigod, they're having the Blind All Stars and Claude Jeter next month, and after that, Sister Rosetta Tharpe!'

The other church, Baptist, across the street from us, was more staid and established: from the window of the bedroom I shared with Lenny, I would stare down every Sunday at the dignified black parishioners, the men in dark suits, the women in cheerful white dresses and splendiferous hats, lingering sociably on the iron balustrade, in a manner I would now characterize as Southern. They represented normalcy to me (an attribute in short supply in our household). I see that the indispensable *AIA Guide to New York City* has deemed that very church across the street architecturally noteworthy: '1860. Ebenezer L. Roberts. A pinch of Lombardian Romanesque decorates a highly articulated square-turreted English Gothic body. The brownstone water tables (white-painted) against red brick are perhaps too harsh.' Picky, picky. I've since become fairly interested in architecture, but as a child I never thought to notice and had no clue back then that the Fort Greene neighborhood around me, which I took to be a dilapidated slum, was actually quite handsome and distinguished, awash in 'Romanesque beauties', as the *AIA Guide* put it. Perhaps all those fieldstone mansions and bay-windowed brownstones, those granite pediments, cylindrical turrets and mansards registered subconsciously, planting the seeds for my later architectural interest; but my reality growing up was much more class-bound. We were barely scraping by, and we stuck out as downwardly mobile whites in a black section that seemed mostly impoverished (although, even then, the area drew a nucleus of home-owning, middle-class black professionals).

Back then, we thought of ourselves as living on the border of Bedford-Stuyvesant, a notoriously rough neighborhood over whose turf two mighty street gangs, the Bishops and the Chaplains, rumbled. I had to be careful where I walked because I would be shaken down by roving bands of kids when I strayed beyond the streets where I was recognized. They would suddenly form a line in front of me. The curious thing was that sometimes they would let me pass, if I said the right thing, pressed the right button, sounded neither too fearful nor too flippant, but sufficiently respectful; they would laugh and say, 'We was just playing with you,' and let me by. Other times they took every penny I had. It didn't have to be a violent encounter if you played it right: more like a loan to a neighbor you knew would never be paid back.

Getting robbed was a straightforward transaction, almost preferable to the teasing, ominous game of 'What you lookin' at?' You had to answer 'Nothing' (or 'You' if you were feeling suicidally cocky: I never was). But even 'Nothing' would not necessarily let you off the hook. You might be told you were lying, you had been seen looking at them, and they might now smash your face in. It was always on the tip of my tongue to ask, not out of provocation but curiosity, 'What if I had been looking at you? What would it mean?' It was mysterious how I could be harming anyone by my gaze. Was it like the aborigine's dread of being photographed? Or like a king whose subjects were forbidden to look upon his splendor? If you did not finesse the response correctly, you might be drawn into a fistfight. The whole point of the exercise was to challenge one's honor. Though I considered my honor not worth a thrashing, and regularly refused to take offense at the dozens of players' slights to my mother's virtue, my situation was complicated by the fact that I did love to look at people. I always felt guilty because I probably *had* been staring at the boy who called me out.

I learned the art of cowardice partly by watching Lenny, and deciding to do the opposite. One memory remains particularly vivid. Lenny and I had entered the vestibule of our apartment building, where they buzz you in. Standing in front of the doorbells was Pete, the toughest kid on the block. Everyone, adult and child, feared Pete. Even in idleness, his body conveyed a coiled power, with the muscular shoulders of a professional prizefighter. His skin was coal black, his bullet head was completely smooth: if he butted you with his skull alone it might knock you out.

'What you lookin at?' he said to my brother, baring his teeth in an almost friendly, ingratiating grin.

'Nothing, okay?'

My brother tried to get past him and put the key in the lock. Pete blocked his way. 'I saw you starin at me. Why you lookin at me? You some kind of fairy? Don't lie. Be a man. Admit you was lookin at me.'

I want to say, Come on, Lenny, tell him you're a fairy, apologize, whatever he wants, just get us to the other side of the door.

Instead Lenny answers, in a heated voice (I know his temper so well): 'Okay, I was looking at you. What of it?'

'You want to fight?' Pete asks tantalizingly, beckoning Lenny forward with his curled hand. It's an invitation, almost like 'You want to dance?' He thrusts his index finger against my brother's chest. My brother raises his fists in the time-honored manner. *Meshugana.*

'Lenny, don't fight him! Come on!'

Neither pays attention to me. Pete grabs him, fast as a cat, before Lenny can change his mind, and they tangle. Lenny's glasses fall to the tiled floor. I grab them and put them in my pocket. My brother is taller than Pete, and tries to tie him up with his long arms, but the tussle lasts only a matter of seconds before Pete breaks away and throws a combination of expert jabs at Lenny's face. My brother goes down. Pete is on him instantly, straddling him, punching him in the face, moving his fist straight down like a pile driver on Lenny's nose. I am thinking, I must save my brother, I must save my brother. I start beating Pete on the back. My arms have an eerie lassitude, my punches lack force. Pete shoves me against the wall with one arm, while the other continues to pummel Lenny. My brother's nose is gushing blood. I start to scream: '*Help!* Stop them!' Maybe someone bigger can break up the fight. Pete starts banging my brother's head against the hard tile floor. This is the worst part. I can only watch, with a sick feeling. Lenny's face is all pink, his eyes are weirdly glassy. Each time his head hits the stone floor with a thud, I register the pain. We're very close, Lenny and I: what happens to one, the other feels. At the same time, some little part of me is glad to see my brother, the tyrant of my youth, getting it. See, idiot, you shouldn't have accepted his challenge. I admire Pete, or at least his ability to fight, even as I am horrified by his lack of emotion. He seems to show no personal malice toward my brother, doesn't even know him, this is just his way of enjoying himself – beating up a white boy. Or bloodying a black boy, on a slow afternoon.

'You'll kill him! *Quit it!*' I'm yelling. An adult, Mack, the super, runs in. Pete rises with a smile, and hold his hands out, as if to say, I'm clean. He darts out the door smooth as a leopard, disappears.

I help my brother up. 'I'm so sorry, Lenny. I couldn't stop him. Are you all right?'

'I'm all right. Motherfucking sonofabitch!'

'Here are your glasses.'

'Next time I'll kill him,' says my brother.

—

Of the three white tenants, besides ourselves, in the building, two were a highly cultivated foreign couple, the man a professor of Spanish, I seem to recall, who spent part of each year in Peru and took an interest in Inca handicrafts. You would have thought that such a refined pair, who read good books and appreciated classical music, would have been a godsend to my parents, who did the same. But not only did we never make friends with them, we ridiculed them behind their backs. The woman, Tina, was rumored to have been caught sun worshiping on the roof, naked to the waist and raising her arms to the sky. She was probably just practicing yoga. As often as I sneaked up to the tarred roof to catch her in this rite, I never saw her doing anything but innocently drawing in her notebook.

Since the singer Yma Sumac had made a big splash with her exotic, scale-ascending vocals, my sister Betty Ann, who was our unofficial bestower of nicknames, dubbed Tina 'Yma'.

I thought Yma harmless, but I was terrified of the other white woman in the building. She lived with our black superintendent, Mack, so we called her Mrs Mack for starters, but later, thanks to Betty Ann, the Dragon Lady, because she smoked constantly and curled the smoke up her nose, and because she had a surly, evil expression, with tiny, mistrustful eyes embedded in a porcine face rolling in fat, and huge, dimpled arms that she used to lean on, while looking out the window for Mack. She would chase us kids away when we tried to throw a pink Spaldeen ball against the cornice beneath her window. She always wore the same faded housedresses, and gave off a strong, oniony body odor. Since Mack himself was a patient, decent-looking, squat, muscular man who tolerated children and in consequence was well-liked by them, we wondered how he could have gotten stuck with such a repulsive sow. It was said that some black men had a 'thing' for white women, but surely her skin color alone could not have balanced out her other defects. Yet there seemed an undeniable physical passion between them, a powerful glue; you sensed it when you saw them together.

I could certainly understand the attraction white women might feel toward black men. I looked up to blacks also, as a rule: it was the beginning of my White

Negro period, and I had no difficulty romanticizing them as a superior race. Their best seemed stoically graceful and effortlessly creative, like our neighbor across the hall, Melville, who was a track star at Boys' High School and an honor student, outrageously handsome, with the friendly, obliging manner of a natural-born aristocrat. My boyhood heroes had been the Dodgers' Jackie Robinson and Don Newcombe. By the time I was twelve, my brother had introduced me to rhythm and blues; we would thrill to Mickey & Sylvia and Sam 'The Man' Taylor on the radio, and from there it was but a short step to worshiping Charlie Parker, John Coltrane, Bessie Smith, and the blind gospel singers.

One day Lenny came home all excited. He had just learned that the drunk we sometimes stumbled over near the corner of our block, where Washington Avenue and Fulton Street met, the wino who slept in the alley beside the gospel church, was none other than Gil Coggins, a former bop piano player who had once recorded with Bird! My brother, who usually responded with ironic grimaces when misfortunes fell on our own family, was so touched at and angered by the fate of this black musician, at how American society undervalued its jazz artists and permitted them to end up in the gutter. He vowed to do something about it. What? I was curious to know. At the very least he would talk to the man, tell how much his music had meant to him. (For my part, after that I never came upon the sleeping ex-sideman without reverently tiptoeing around him.)

There was a difference, of course, between the demigods and the everyday blacks you came across, who might stare you down with a scowl, but here, too, I made my adjustments. After I'd lived on the block a while, it seemed to me my neighbors knew who I was, and either accepted me or just left me alone. The row of brownstones next to the Baptist church made a perfect backdrop for punchball – there was just enough room from end to end to hit a decent-size fly ball for a homer – and the black kids who lived there would let me into their games if they were short of players. 'Easy out,' they would taunt me. I would bunch my fist together, pretending it had the hard, bony strength of theirs. To hit a punchball far does not require massive biceps: you toss the ball up and whack it with your fist. There is a knack in the wrist, or the knuckles, which I never quite mastered, though sometimes I got lucky.

But then, just as I thought I was becoming invisible, or that race didn't matter, I would be brought up short. As I loved to sing, I had joined a Hebrew choir when my family lived in Williamsburg, continuing to perform in it after my family moved to Fort Greene. One night I was coming home from a gig at a Bronx synagogue. This was just before my own bar mitzvah; I was twelve. Though it was late, I decided to walk the mile from Fulton Street and Franklin Avenue, rather than make the several train transfers which would have put me a block from home. Franklin Avenue was an elevated train station: at the bottom of the steps awaited the one corner I was afraid of, a seedy intersection that felt menacing even on ordinary nights.

This particular night, there was a crowd at the foot of the El steps, listening to an angry black orator. He stood on a makeshift raised platform decorated with signs for the U.S. Labor Party, a Communist front. Usually I liked crowds; I trusted them, I was curious about speechmakers. But this crowd had a nasty growl to it. The orator was whipping them up about Emmett Till, the boy who had just been lynched down South. I knew about the case, because my liberal parents talked about it often; we were outraged at the bigots who had lynched Emmett Till. But suddenly that didn't matter: I had to traverse a semicircle around the crowd, making myself inconspicuous, before I could continue down Fulton Street.

'Now they took that twelve-year-old Negro boy and strung him up and choked the sweet life out of him, just because they *saaaid* . . . said he looked at a white woman. Said he *looked* at a white woman. And our government sits by, don't do a thing. Not a thing. So I ask you. What are you going to do about it? What you gonna do about it?'

Everyone started yelling for revenge. I tried to make myself small, harmless, childlike. The thought struck me that I was about the same age as Emmett Till. An eye for an eye. I began inching my way behind the crowd, as silently as I could, when suddenly some voices started yelling, 'Hey, here's one!'

'Look at that white devil!'

'He got some nerve comin round here.'

'Leave him alone,' growled the speaker. 'He just a kid.'

'Emmett Till just a kid!' responded someone.

'Our conflict is with the ones in power. Let us not confuse the issue,' the speaker said wearily. The crowd turned back to listen. I scurried up the street. He had saved my skin – whether out of compassion or ideological purity I would never know.

—

I had lived on Washington Avenue for three years, and was approaching fourteen, when a new white family moved into the building. By that time we had made casual friendships with many neighbors, and almost resented the presence of this new white contingent, who, we felt obscurely, had no business being here. You would think we wanted to shut the door after us and keep the neighborhood from tipping. But it was rather that, like typical American Jews, we had assimilated – albeit to a black ghetto – and the fact that these newcomers were Jews who spoke with a heavy Polish accent, looking like they'd just come fresh off the boat, made us uncomfortable. They would draw attention to our being Jewish, to the whole idea of Jewishness.

Sure enough, the Januschеs were delighted when, after probing my mother in the hallway, they found out we were Jewish. Too delighted, for my taste.

Confirming my worst fears, they remarked about the '*schwarzes*' around us not knowing how to 'keep clean'. Occasionally I saw the newcomers in the darkened, orange-walled lobby, entering while I was leaving. Mr Janusch, a bone-slender man with a mustache, who wore a suit, tie, fedora, and topcoat, even in balmy weather; his stout wife, who seemed always to be bossing her husband, and Georgie, their pudgy ten-year-old. The boy spoke reluctantly to his mother in Polish, but whenever he saw some other kid coming, he would break out a very American whine, 'Oh, Ma!'

After a few months, I got the peculiar impression that Mrs Janusch was studying me. Why, I had no idea, but whenever our paths crossed she would eye me with a quick, shrewd look. She had a penchant for black fur collars and feathery ruffs, which set off her chubby but not unpretty face in the manner of middle-period Elizabeth Taylor. Her jetblack eyes flashed imperiously, as though she were used to giving orders in the Old Country. My sister Betty Ann had immediately dubbed her 'the Polish Countess'.

One day, as I was getting the mail, Mrs Janusch pounced on me from nowhere.

'Excuse me, you go to *chader*?' she asked, using the Yiddish word for Hebrew school.

'Not anymore. I had my bar mitzvah a year ago,' I said, blushing. 'I go once a week to a Bible discussion group for kids who have been bar mitzvahed.'

'And do you lay *tefillin*?' she asked, referring to

the morning devotional prayers with leather phylacteries which are the duty of young Jewish men.

'Sometimes. Not so much lately.'

'But you read Hebrew well. Your mother tells me you were in a Hebrew choir?'

'Yes, until a little while ago,' I said, flattered that she should know that. 'What did you do in the choir?'

'I – sang during the High Holidays, and at weddings, bar mitzvahs, concerts.'

'And why did you quit?' she asked keenly.

'I got tired of it,' I lied. The truth was, my voice had changed with puberty, and besides, I resented the fact that I never got more solos. I had sounded too 'American' for the choir leader to feature me; I didn't have that plaintive *shtetl* melisma.

'Everyone around here says you're very smart.'

'Around here. . . .'

'Don't deny it. You know my son, George? Do you think you could teach him to read Hebrew? He knows the letters already, but . . . either he is too slow or he just doesn't bother. His father is ashamed that he can't take him to *shul* with him.'

'I don't understand Hebrew either. Just a few dozen words.'

'But you read it fast, yes? That's all his father wants. Besides, Georgie likes you.'

'How can you tell? We've never even had a conversation.'

'I can tell the way he looks at you. Mothers know.

How do you say in English? "He looks up to you." If *you* teach him to read Hebrew, George will be interested.'

'I'm not sure how to do it. I've never taught before.'

'Think about it. I will speak to your mother. I will pay, of course.'

She worked out a deal with my mother. I would get $2.50 a week to tutor Georgie, and, since summer vacation was about to start, Betty Ann would also get paid two dollars to make his lunch on weekdays. Two-fifty was good money for me in those days – two and a half times my weekly allowance. The choir had only paid me twenty-five dollars a year; I could make that now in ten weeks. Besides, the idea of teaching appealed to me. At school I loved to stand in front of the class and deliver a report or recite a poem. Aside from my tiresome need to show off, I had, even at that early point, a genuine pedagogic urge, which would someday lead me to a teaching career. But I was still uncertain how to go about it. Should I prepare lessons in Hebrew, use learning games? I didn't know any. I would have to bluff – a thought that planted butterflies in my stomach.

My first lesson was scheduled for a Sunday afternoon. The Janusches had asked me to come at four, but they were still finishing off their midday roast when I arrived, so they asked me to wait in the boarder's room for ten minutes. This was a small room at the end of the hall, which they had rented out to an elderly tailor. Every Sunday he went to visit his sister in a nursing home in Queens. The room had an odor of stacked dust and incontinence. On the floor were black socks rolled into balls, brown cardboard suitcases, prayer books, fabric remnant books, used tea glasses, and recent Yiddish newspapers. I occupied myself trying to puzzle out the headlines and captions on the front page. 'La-zar Ka-gano-vitch,' I translated into English the Yiddish letters below the photograph of Kremlin chiefs stiffly reviewing a military parade. Whether the Yiddish daily's slant was pro- or anti-Soviet I couldn't tell; only that it was printed in New York City and fascinated with Russia.

The room's disheveled condition stood in marked contrast to the rest of the apartment, which was immaculate, the oak or mahogany furniture highly polished, the inlaid parquet floors spotless. Yet the Janusches had suggested that the first lesson take place in the boarder's room: I wondered why. Perhaps they wanted to spare Georgie the embarrassment of their looking on. Too, the room did have the appropriately musty air of a synagogue back room.

I was sunk deep in a scratchy velveteen chair of a faded rose color, with dusky splotches where the fabric had been rubbed against the grain, when Georgie entered. I immediately stood up, closed the door behind him, and handed him a prayer book from the floor. 'Read this.' I pointed to a passage. He looked at me with imploring eyes, as though about to be dragged to the slaughterhouse. I was calm but stern: if anything, his fear reassured me and quickened my sense of power, making me feel less like a fraud. He began stumbling through the first syllables. Right then, I decided to spend the first few sessions simply listening to him read and gauging his level – the old diagnostic-stall maneuver, which all teachers in the dark employ. His forehead beaded with sweat as he read. I put my hand on his shoulder. 'Start again. This time read just the first paragraph. Slowly, don't rush it.'

He began again, and I corrected each of his mistakes in a neutral voice, while looking over his shoulder. He would bite his lip when he stumbled, or punch his arm, muttering 'Dummy'. He was making mistakes more from nerves than from ignorance. I knew I would have to reduce his level of fear somehow. My strategy was to get him to read one paragraph perfectly, build up his confidence this way, then move on to the next. The inspiration that struck me during the first lesson was very simple: all he needs is practice.

By the end of the hour, he could read the first three paragraphs of the daily prayer. I returned him to his parents. I don't know whether or not they had been listening at the door, but they greeted us with pleased expressions. Georgie's piglet eyes gleamed shiny yet sleepy. 'Now can I play outside?' he demanded. His mother kissed him on his blond, cropped head. Then she squeezed his cheeks together and yanked his face up to her lips, giving him a real mother-son smooch. The quiet Mr Janusch smiled his gold-toothed smile and looked away apologetically.

—

The Januschés lived two flights below us, so that it was possible for Betty Ann to stick her head out the window of their apartment and call up the courtyard shaft, 'Phee-lips! Gee-orge is ready for you,' in a thick Polish accent, mimicking the Countess's mispronunciations. I would put down my library book (that summer I was making my way through *100 American Plays*, encountering for the first time the suave humor of George S. Kaufman and Philip Barry, planets remote from Fort Greene, Brooklyn) and run downstairs, where Georgie would have just finished his lunch, typically a grilled cheese sandwich and tomato soup. Betty Ann, good sister that she was, often left an extra lunch for me.

I was fired with ambition now to make George into a smooth, rapid reader of Hebrew. I had visions of his being called up to the Torah and impressing everyone. 'Who is that little kid?' they would say. 'Where did he learn to read so well?' But his progress was less than astonishing. Without his parents in the next room, Georgie proved harder to control – I practically had to sit on him to keep him in one place. The kid was sly and used every delaying device he could.

We would begin by chatting for a few minutes. It was then that Georgie would do his damnedest to undercut the lesson, through a combination of coyness and mischief. 'Oh please?' he would beg, pressing his fingers together in a steeple.

'That's the Christian sign of prayer – that won't do you any good here. Come on, get in the other room,' I'd say. Next he would try to make me chase him: daring me, he would dart toward my reach and spin away. Admittedly, Georgie was not very fast, but sometimes he could squirm out of my grasp like the greased little piglet he was. He seemed to crave rough-and-tumble physical contact with an older male; perhaps he never got enough of that from his father. His clownishness made me laugh against my will, and he used it to his advantage to stall (just as, I suppose, I used his liking for me to make him study). Other times, my amusement at him vanished without a trace, usually when he was being a little too cute or coy. Such maneuvers might charm an adult but they would fail to work on another child.

If Georgie sometimes miscalculated by forgetting I was still a child, he remembered it enough to exploit my secret weakness: that I also wanted to play. I had made the mistake one day of taking him outside for a game of punchball after he had done particularly well with his lessons. After that it was always: 'Aw, why can't we just skip Hebrew this time and play punchball? I won't tell, I promise.' Instantly, the nerves in my punchball arm quivered, as I imagined belting a pink ball down the block. 'No, we have to study.'

We eventually struck an arrangement. I would use the punchball game as a carrot to keep him, the donkey, praying. If he read x number of pages without a single mistake, we could cut ten minutes off the end of the lesson. A few times, however, I gave in to temptation and we went outside to play before our goals had been met. We would try to scare up a game with whichever kids happened to be in the vicinity. If there weren't enough players for two punchball squads, we would resort to three-box baseball or hit the dime. One reason Georgie was so keen on our playing outside together was that I protected him. He had already acquired a reputation on the block for being both obnoxious and defenseless. A chunky kid who tried to whine his way into every game, he seemed a walking invitation for a stiff punch. Betty Ann joked that we were really getting paid to see that the kid didn't get beat up. There was some truth in that: since Georgie was lonely and friendless, his mother had in effect hired him a couple of companions.

—

The synagogue for which I was preparing Georgie, the Fort Greene Jewish Center, was housed in a dignified, red-stone Romanesque structure with a pointed roof and stained-glass windows. The congregation, a droplet of Orthodox Jewry in an indifferent ocean, had been forced to rent an old, abandoned church until such time as it could muster the resources to build a new synagogue. (It seems that the building has returned to use as a church, since the sign outside it today says 'Eglise Haitienne'.)

I usually entered the synagogue through the back door, which was a block closer to my house and opened onto a gymnasium, the unofficial domain of us teenagers. Here the Saturday-night socials for teens were held: a phonograph with a felt turntable would sit on a folding chair, and I would station myself by it, pretending that monitoring the choice of 45 rpm records engrossed me too much to dance, while the other boys tried to feel up the more precocious twelve-year-old girls. Here also the Boy Scouts met. I had gone to only one meeting of the troop's chapter, and, turned off by the unsupervised rowdiness, all these doltish Jewish boys wrestling each other sadistically on the floor, I sneaked out when no one was looking. The gym was also where the kiddush of wine and honey cake and sometimes herring was set out, on folding tables with white tablecloths, after bar mitzvahs.

You had to cross the lengthy gymnasium, with its basketball hoops, sports equipment cartons, and folded bingo tables, to enter the synagogue proper. But once there, you came upon the Old World. It was a happy accident that the church interior had duplicated the classical architecture of Eastern European synagogues: the carved wooden railings, the steps leading to the raised ark in the middle, the balconies reserved for women and girls, all of which had a curiously nautical flavor, like the deck of a clipper ship. The old men in the front benches would chant in hoarse singsong the first words of a prayer, such as '*Ashro yishraw v'seycha*', then rock back and forth in their ancient bobbing motion, *davening*, mumbling the rest under their breaths. It was these old men who were the spiritual (though not the socioeconomic) heart of the community. They kept an eye on tradition, and would grumble at the little mistakes Rabbi Dorfman, just turned forty, made in the service, or criticize his upbeat, patriotic sermons. I shared their contempt for this nasal-voiced, smiling rabbi, with his seminary vocabulary: 'Let us now partake of the repast.' But the old men were no kinder to me. At my bar mitzvah, when I had not only chanted the traditional *haftorah* portion but led the whole morning service, having learned the routine in my Hebrew choir, and there was even some talk around the congregation of their using me in future as a boy cantor (to save money they would otherwise have to spend hiring an outside cantor), and I was accepting compliments all around, two of the elders crooked their fingers at me and said I should not have repeated a certain phrase more than twice, it was a sin! They knew.

These old men were small and wrinkled as dwarfs, and they seemed to have nothing to do with America. I liked them for that, and for the furious looks they gave us boys who breathlessly entered from the gym during morning service, causing the leather doors to creak. (You were supposed to stand waiting and look through the diamond-shaped window cut into the door, and only enter during a break in the service.) Except for a few grandfathers who grinned toothlessly at anything young, most of these old worshipers showed no sentimentality toward children. Perhaps because they were equally small, they felt endangered by these wild beasts that showed no reverence for the Law.

From my favorite pew, last row right, where I could watch everyone who was seated in the balcony, especially a girl I liked, Merrily Waxman, without being seen myself, I would find myself drawn to the old men and wonder what consoling thoughts collected in their minds while they read the same prayers that left me cold. I wanted to believe in God and the rest, the way they did. But all that incomprehensible Hebrew did nothing for me, and the English translation facing it was no better: incessant praise for an Almighty Deity who seemed to need to be flattered and told all the time how great He was. I knew this was not the only way to think about my religion, but it was too late, I was on the slippery slope of disbelief.

And yet I kept coming back to the synagogue. No one forced me to – certainly not my parents, who told me even on the High Holidays, 'You can go, it's not for us, honey.' Or my older brother, who was already proudly calling himself an atheist. But the year after a young man undergoes a bar mitzvah is a crucial time, in which he is specifically instructed to strengthen his faith. Precisely because I was no longer strapped to the conveyor belt of bar mitzvah lessons, and my participation was voluntary, it seemed to me I was duty-bound to try. I rose a few times at dawn and lashed the leather thongs of the phylacteries around my wrists and read the morning prayers. The upshot was that I felt embarrassed, as though I were attempting to acquire the mindset of a nomadic shepherd in opposition to the modern world.

Only in the synagogue did I not feel embarrassed about practicing Judaism. There I felt bored, but that seemed appropriate: everyone else was. And sometimes a mysterious shiver went through me when I put on the *tallis*, the ceremonial striped shawl; I felt a warmth which issued from more than the thin weight of the cloth. I instantly became more stoop-shouldered under that silken pressure, as though bypassing manhood and progressing straight to a pious, bent old age. When the Torah was paraded around the synagogue, I scrambled like everyone else to touch it, kissing the shawl's fringes to my lips and pressing them against the holy scroll as it marched past my aisle. I was kissing God.

—

At other times, the Jewish ritual meant nothing to me. Why was I drilling Georgie in sight-reading Hebrew? It seemed so mechanical, this skill of reading Hebrew rapidly without mistakes. What did he need it for? As far as I could tell, his parents were not particularly religious; they didn't even light Sabbath candles.

Receiving my wages one week, I noticed that Mrs Janusch, in her black orchid summer dress, had numbers on her arms. It didn't particularly surprise me: ever since I was a small boy, Brooklyn had accumulated those who had been in the concentration camps. You would go into a hardware store and the man behind the counter would be gruff and ill-tempered, and you'd notice the numbers on his arm. The Polish Countess was not that sour type, but she was somewhat adamant. In any case, after this discovery it began to make sense to me that she would want her son to know how to carry himself as a Jew, having paid such a steep price for it herself.

Each time Mrs Janusch counted my wages, she tried to lure me into a heart-to-heart talk about George's progress.

'Do you think he's slow?' she'd ask.

'He's all right. He's getting it.'

'But he's lazy. He doesn't practice when you're not here. I wonder if he has the brains to amount to anything. No, it's not brains, that isn't the problem –'

'Certainly not, he's a smart kid.'

'You mustn't think because intelligence comes easy to you,' she said, 'that it is the same for everyone.'

I blushed. I wasn't being modest; I certainly thought I was smarter than her son. But she should not have been the one to tell me that. Why all these interrogations about Georgie? Leave the kid alone, I thought. What I didn't understand was that her constant parental concern masked her adoration of him. It was one more opportunity to talk about her beloved child. I misread it as a sort of flirtation passing between her and me. I resented her way of cornering me, especially as I found her, in spite of my initial impressions, attractive. My youthful tendency to caricature all adults as grotesque told me that she was a fat, silly foreigner; but my fourteen-year-old eyes kept being drawn to her bosom. And she would give me these shrewd, penetrating looks. It all comes back to me, the terror of that deep, probing look her woman's eyes imposed on me as a boy.

The one time Mrs Janusch crossed the line was when she told me I was my mother's favorite. It shamed me to hear this woman, this outsider, calmly put into words what I had long suspected but dared not believe, in loyalty to my siblings; in fact, I rejected the claim with all my might. Far from feeling honored, I held it deeply against Mrs Janusch for her invasive picking at that Oedipal thread.

—

One day, Georgie and I were taking a breather from reading Hebrew by going over some Bible stories. I had just read aloud the one about Joshua praying to have the sun stop in the sky, when Georgie said: 'That's impossible. That's a cock-and-bull story.'

'Why do you say that?'

'Because, if the sun stopped, everything would fall

off the earth and we'd all be dead. Joshua would be dead, too.' My pupil seemed so proud of his cleverness I had to smile.

'Maybe it is scientifically impossible. But don't you think that if God wanted to, He could do something that was scientifically impossible?'

'No, because that's what *impossible* means. It can't be done.'

'Except in the case of miracles,' I said impishly.

Georgie looked stymied. 'I don't get it. You're gonna tell me – ?'

'Look, we read in the Bible that the earth was created in six days. Scientists like Darwin say that's impossible. So there are two explanations. One is that if you believe God is all-powerful, He could do anything He wants. He could have made the earth in six days, and He could have strewn fossils around that looked like they came from millions of years apart. I'm not saying He did, but He could have. The other explanation is that each of those six days stood for so many thousands or millions of years. So the Bible tells the truth, but in a roundabout way.'

'I get a beating when I do that.'

'It's not a fib. It's a code. The Bible substitutes one thing for another. Six days means six million years. Maybe making the sun stop is code for an eclipse. Everyone got confused in the midst of battle, thinking Joshua had made the sun disappear.'

'So which is right, the miracle or the eclipse?'

'That's for you to choose.'

'You're the teacher, you're supposed to tell me. I'm just the smart-aleck kid.'

'I don't know what the answer is. I wasn't around at the time.'

'The way I see it, a code is just another way of saying it's a cock-and-bull story.'

'You love that expression, don't you?'

Georgie's challenging of the Joshua story pleased me. Essentially I agreed with him, though my own doubts about the Bible arose less from scientific contradiction than from moral concerns: the stories where God came off acting like a bully. For instance, Sodom and Gomorrah: why wouldn't God go along with Abraham's plea for mercy? I had thrashed this out in one session of the study group for post-bar mitzvah kids at the Fort Greene Jewish Center. These discussions were conducted by Max Drucker, a somber, intelligent man with silver hair and a pencil mustache, whose leg wound in World War II forced him to limp with pain. It was Drucker who had suggested to my parents that I become a cantor. First, because I had a good singing voice, and, second, because cantors did not have to fight in wars but could serve on the sidelines, like chaplains. This perk did not seem to me a sufficient career motivation. But I was touched that he had thought enough of me to make the suggestion. Maybe because he did like me and I respected his learning, I took it upon myself to argue with him at every session.

Drucker listened patiently. He was the kind of intellectual opponent who conveys the impression that, for all his seeming openness, it is only a matter of time before you give in to his superior reason. He was stubborn; I was, too. The difference was that when it came to Judaism, he knew what he was talking about and I didn't.

'Mr Drucker, maybe the grown-ups in Sodom and Gomorrah were bad, but I don't think God should have destroyed the babies or the little children, when they were just copying their parents.'

'You are saying that environment influences behavior,' said Drucker. 'But does that excuse it?'

'Well, if you come from a long line of family members who see evil as normal, you probably act evil, just to fit in. Couldn't God understand that?'

'It is not a question of God's understanding. God understands all. But let us discuss *your* understanding for the moment. Yes, we are shaped by environment, but also we are responsible for our actions. Into each person God puts a *seed*, an awareness of good and evil. We are given free will, which differentiates us from machines, and it is up to each of us to follow the good.'

'But doesn't it take a while for that awareness to develop? And in the case of babies or small children, why didn't God give them a decent chance?'

'It is not for us to sit in judgment of God's actions. If God destroyed Sodom and Gomorrah, He must have been convinced that the people in it were past redemption.'

'But why does God see people in such black and white terms?' I persisted. 'Most people are a combination of good and bad.'

'Some people are evil,' said Drucker, seeming to speak from experience.

'But God made the world, so He made the evil in it, too. It must have been part of His plan for those Sodom and Gommorahites to be bad in the first place.'

'No. He gave them a choice, and they chose to ignore Him. To sin and to blaspheme. You see the difference?'

'But if He left evil around in the world as a temptation, and then made man into a creature who was too weak to refuse, then it was a foregone conclusion that man would fall into the trap.'

'You and I are talking about two different things here. I am not discussing how evil came to be in the world, which is an interesting theological problem for some other time, but specifically Sodom and Gomorrah, a place where men and women not only fell into the trap but fell up to their ears. They were extraordinarily evil. And without exception. Let me give you an example closer to home. Your argument reminds me of the Nuremberg trials. After World War II ended, the biggest Nazi criminals were rounded up and put on trial.' He paused for effect. I nodded, tired of this analogy: in postwar Jewish Brooklyn, every minor infraction led straight to Buchenwald. 'And after they got through pointing fingers at each other, which was a nauseating spectacle in and of itself, they all came up with the same excuse: 'We were just following orders.' They were just conforming to the 'normal', to use your word, behavior in Nazi Germany. I remember one of them even testified that if there had been protests from the ordinary German people, they might have thought twice – but nobody raised a word of protest. This Nazi officer was trying to say that, in an environment where everyone is guilty, no one is guilty. That is a common misconception. In fact the opposite is true. In an environment where everyone is guilty, *everyone* should be punished!' Here, Drucker turned red in the face and raised his voice. 'Only in that way can we have justice. And that is the meaning of God's destruction of Sodom and Gomorrah.'

All this time the other post-bar mitzvah boys, who came every week, perhaps because their parents badgered them or because they liked to play basketball afterward in the gym, looked on resentfully at our duel. They thought Drucker was a gimpy wheeze bag, and I a smart-ass showoff. They would have been surprised to know how much it pained me to rip holes in my faith, how much I wished I could have been one of them.

—

By September, Georgie had become fluent enough at reading Hebrew for me to bring him to synagogue, where he was called to the Torah and read aloud passably for two minutes, during a special Young

People's part of the service. His parents were so pleased that they urged me to continue teaching him Hebrew (a language I still insisted I did not know) and, additionally, to help him with spelling, one of his poorer subjects. I was glad for the chance to diversify my pedagogic repertoire.

For an hour each afternoon, after the regular school day, I would enter the Janusches' clean, dust-free apartment. Sometimes Georgie would be hiding, and would leap out at me. Georgie's success at the Torah service had changed him, made him cockier. 'It's a snap,' he would say when I reproached him for not trying enough, and I let him coast for a while.

With the colder weather, a new craze began: marbles. It started on a rainy day. Punchball being out of the question, Georgie took out his marble set after the lesson, and I fell in with him. I had never gone in for marbles when I was his age, so their charm lay ready to hit me full force. There were black agates, eerie and formal as obsidian, and gray-green combinations the color of cats' eyes, and smoky whites, clouded over like cataracts, and one pure purple.

I loved getting down on my knees with Georgie and matching him shot for shot. The basic idea was to be the first to reach certain destination points – the dining room table leg, the fourth parquet tile, the standing lamp – while knocking out, as in croquet, the opponent's marbles. But we kept making up more elaborate rules. The dining room floor was our playing field, and we spent much of the game under the oak dining table, with whose leaves and brackets I became well-acquainted. The room looked different from this vantage point: we had turned its stuffy order into a shooting range. From sheer rambunctiousness we would send marbles flying under the radiator or even into the bedroom of his parents, which we were expressly forbidden to enter. A sliding door separated the dining room from the bedroom, and when it was left open, a marble would sometimes get stuck in the runner's grooves, or bounce merrily past and roll under the bed. Were we to lose it and should his parents happen to find it there, Georgie warned, 'We would be in biiiiiiig trouble.'

I knew I was forfeiting dignity and moral authority in scrambling around after my tutee on all fours. But perhaps this is why I liked the game: it equalized us. We had marble tournaments that went on for hours, and, once the sport had gotten into my blood, there were days when temptation led me to suspend lessons altogether. This was a serious mistake: I was giving Georgie ammunition for snitching on me. Nor did I like the aftertaste of forgoing my duties and cheating my employers. But the game held such seductive power over me that Georgie knew he had only to propose marbles for my will to buckle. That fall I lived for marbles, their neutral temperature and lightness in my hand, the skill involved in controlling length and curve of flight with a finger flick, their resemblance to cut diamonds or other colorful jewel stones, the hilarious way they kept rolling and ending up in unforeseen places, their momentum and resilience, like a cartoon character falling off a cliff and dusting himself off, seemingly indestructible, all the more curious in that they were made of glass.

I sensed myself entering a morally confused zone where the rules were becoming too flexible, and might ultimately undermine my ability to control my student. What complicated the issue of discipline was that Georgie's behavior seemed to be undergoing a change for the worse. Every day his speech grew more vulgar and full of TV clichés, perhaps mimicking his schoolmates': he had the immigrant's quick ear for slang, the child's need to adapt socially, and would imitate Porky Pig or Bugs Bunny by the hour, until I wanted to thrash him. If I told him to read a page in Hebrew, his first response was likely to be 'Thuffering thuccatash!'

'Come on, be serious,' I'd say.

'B-b-b-biya, b-bibiya, bibya. That's all, folks!'

He would latch on to a phrase like 'Duck, you sucker!' and use it every minute, the way a small child repeats a potty word just to get on your nerves. He became devoted to pig Latin: everything was 'ouyay antcay', and so on. 'Shoot, Sarge!' was another of his pet sayings, spoken with a lisp, as a coy way to avoid my teaching demands. If I had a hard time locating the authentic Georgie underneath these robotic pop-culture quotations, I could not help but appreciate his strategy. All this spewing of lines from cartoons and radio jingles was a clever resistance to after-school tutoring, a revenge for my robbing him of his leisure playtime.

I needed to find other incentives to keep him involved. But instead, I began losing patience with him. My hold on his respect was loosening, and the more saucily he behaved, the more I wanted to slap him into line. The first time I hit him, he was quite surprised. So was I. 'Well, I told you to pick up the book!' I said hotly, hoping my indignant tone would drown out what I had done. It seemed a momentary aberration, one which need never be repeated.

Yet something about his chunky body and squealing laugh made me want to punch him a few days later, and a few days after that. It wasn't only that he was so provoking; in fact, I don't think I ever got angry enough to really paste him. No, basically I liked Georgie, but I just wanted to plant my fist somewhere in his flesh. I have mentioned already what I took to be the boy's hunger for physical roughhousing with an older male, his propensity to come perilously close to me and then wheel away. Well, I discovered much to my surprise that I had a similar longing: to catch the kid and squeeze him in a tight wrestling hug, to graze his head with a noogie (a playful head knuckle), and finally, quite simply, to hurt him. I wonder if it wasn't some sort of sadomasochistic dance on both our parts: he would taunt, I would punch. The same pattern as I had mastered with my older brother, only this time I was the one dealing out blows. One could say in my defense that my whole 'environment', with its imprintings of violence, had taught me to act this way, but what kind of bullshit excuse is that? I was supposed to be the good boy, the smart one. Was this the only way I could attempt to shrug off the premature burdens of grown-up responsibility that had been placed on me, or that I had placed on myself? Another bullshit excuse. Was it my retaliation for Mrs Janusch stigmatizing me as my mother's favorite? Who knows? Each time I lost control and punched Georgie – usually with a swift blow to the arm – I found myself to be a stranger. I was amazed at the brutality surfacing from inside me.

'Don't tell your mother, okay?' I first threatened, then pleaded. He looked at me with a silent, wounded expression, the dark, superior understanding that the abused has of the abuser.

—

My hunch was that he would not tell his mother. In the meantime, in the week that followed, I made a vow never to hit him again. I became tolerance itself in our lessons. Georgie seemed placated; inwardly I rejoiced at my narrow escape. 'Just let me get away with this one thing, Lord,' I prayed to the God of Abraham and Isaac. On Friday, I went down to the Janusch apartment to collect my wages. The Countess had taken off her work clothes, and was sitting at the dining room table in a black slip. Her feet were soaking in a basin of warm water. She looked weary as she counted out the money.

'Georgie tells me that you hit him.'

'I . . . did lose my temper with him once, yes –'

'Not once but several times,' she cut me off. 'I am very disappointed in you.' She looked me hard in the face, to let me understand that, in addition to my sins against Georgie, I had personally violated her trust as well.

What could I say? I agreed completely. 'I'm sorry.'

She nodded. 'You cannot work for us anymore.'

I had prepared myself for some reproach, yet, oddly enough, I had not expected to be fired; such a total break caught me off-balance. It was on the tip of my tongue to ask for another chance, but there was that in me that recognized the justice of her decision. I got up and left.

This passage of my life, this business of teaching Georgie, was really over. In the days that followed I felt sick to my stomach. It was the squeamish guilty sensation that comes from not only knowing you did wrong but knowing that your true nature has been found out. I would encounter that same sensation at various other times in my adult life, when I had to ask myself: how could I have done or said such a cruel thing? I would cringe, I would laugh disbelievingly, to cushion the feeling, and I would never learn a thing from any of it, except that I should not be surprised when some foulness leaps out of me. Like the people in Sodom and Gomorrah, apparently I was one of the evil ones.

## – My Brother the Radio Host –

My brother, Leonard, is a radio personality, heard every weekday in the New York metropolitan area on a midday, two-hour interview show. Being a generalist and a quick study, he ranges widely, questioning novelists, politicians, scientists, film directors, actresses, car mechanics, chefs. I listen as often as I can, not only because he is my brother but because he has, in my opinion, the best show on radio – the most informative, discerning, entertaining. Even knowing him as I do, I am amazed at how astutely he can shape a fifteen-minute or half-hour interview. Of course, knowing him so well, I also am aware when he is bluffing about a subject he has only vague notions about, and I sometimes catch him making errors. I will yell at the radio, 'No no no, Lenny!' when he gets his facts wrong or makes a dubious comment. I am more tolerant of his bad puns; those we love should be permitted their puns.

One of my secret pleasures in listening to him is that I can still hear the unsure but learning-eager adolescent he was at our dinner table, imparting his latest discovery, inside the smooth tones of the all-knowing radio personality. Though he always had a euphonious voice, he has done considerable work on that instrument, shaping its baritone, losing the family's Brooklyn regionalisms. The only aspect of his radio persona that dismays me is when he comes across as dripping with solicitude for some guest, say, who is telling a sob story to flog her memoir; and I sense an insincerity in that momentary delay, that vocal catch (ending questions with 'isn't it?') that has become a signature tic in his delivery. Perhaps because I'm so conscious of how sardonically unsentimental he can be off the air, it is clear to me what a constructed artifact is his radio persona of the patient, empathic listener. It's part of what makes him such a professional.

We are both proud of each other's success – he no less than I. Sometimes as I'm listening to his show I will be brought up short by a reference to his brother the writer. I register that I am in his thoughts as much as he is in mine.

Are we competitive? Of course, as brothers often are. But the roots of our sibling rivalry go far back, and have been overlaid with much self-consciousness on that score. The times I do experience sibling rivalry are when he is not around, and others bring him up. People are constantly pitting us against each other, for either sadistic amusement or experimental curiosity, to see what reactions they can elicit. 'Do you and your brother get along?' they will ask, often with the juicy hope of hearing that we don't. But we do. Lenny is far more well-known in the city than I: a radio personality cannot help but have more fans than an essayist. And the bond a radio talk-show host has with his regular listeners is psychologically complex: not seeing the person but only hearing that mellifluous, sympathetic voice each day invites them to fantasize about and idealize the host. Though I understand this hero-worshiping dynamic, I still don't like it when I am giving a reading at a bookstore and someone's first question is about my brother: that seems tactless, at a moment when I am trying to project an outsize authorial persona. I forgive his radio fans their need to connect with celebrity through me. I have a harder time forgiving my fellow authors, who should know better but only want to talk to me about the last time they were on my brother's show or saw him at a party. I have the urge to say to them: Look, I've written a dozen books, why not spare a few words for my work? But typically they are more interested in my brother's ability to publicize their writing; they come to regard him as a flattering, megaphone extension of their egos.

An awkward moment, too, occurs when I am introduced to someone who says, 'Oh, I love what you do on the radio!' I should take the approach John Ford did when complimented on *Red River*; he would thank them politely and never make the correction that that particular western was directed by Howard Hawks. My brother tells me many people compliment *him* on the books he has ostensibly written. We laugh at this notion that one could be expected to hold down a demanding daily radio show while turning out books. It's as if the public could not be bothered to understand that there are two Lopates, so they keep conflating us.

I also laugh *at* him sometimes, because his renown has given him a touchy sense of self-importance. He does not like to have to wait in line, or produce IDs. If we go to a party together and people do not recognize his name, he will sulk. His way of sulking is to stare high into the middle distance with a frown.

A trickier side to having a radio personality in the family is that he is not always able to come down from his public persona. I become instantly wary of him when I sense that he is not talking to *me* so much as to his listeners, or if I catch him making pronouncements, explaining something he should know I know. (Then again, I should talk: after teaching a seminar or giving several readings on tour, I don't always succeed in descending from Mount Olympus and attending to my wife and daughter on their terms.) With Lenny, I often find myself on guard, cocking my ear for a more private, fraternal tone that should be my due; and if it is not immediately forthcoming, I take umbrage.

In short, I am jealous of our unique connection and do not like to see it diluted. I would rather get together with him for a tête-à-tête than share him with his significant other and friends. Those times when we do see each other alone, going to either a play or a preview screening to which he has invited me, we converse with the old rapport.

I should point out that, for all my antennae-alert mistrust of my brother's outer-directed personality, it is Lenny who shares openly with me his emotional problems or confusions. I tend to be more reserved in those matters, being the younger and, historically, the more intimidated; and I guess I prefer the power of the listener-therapist role, whereas Lenny is much more given to self-dramatization, even if it means being seen as the one in crisis.

For all that, we are, I suppose, quite a lot alike. When we were growing up, we indulged in *The Corsican Brothers* fantasy that whatever happened to one, the other would also feel at the same moment, however much geographical distance separated us. These days, if we don't see each other for a while and then reunite and compare notes on movies, books, music, or current events, we find we've almost always come to the same conclusions. In our adolescence Lenny was my mentor, introducing me to Billie Holiday, Brueghel, and the Dadaists; so it is hardly surprising that, my mind having been formed to some extent by his, we continue to have similar tastes. This very overlap is a source of both comfort and chagrin: I sometimes get impatient with that consensus and yearn for more stimulating disagreement.

The narcissism of small differences: he is three years older, yet more ardent, youthful, risk-taking. He still chases happiness. I always act like the older, graver, more prudent one, giving advice. He likes fine wines and gourmet food, is something of an epicurean. I, more of a stoic, can appreciate a well-cooked meal but will not go miles out of my way for one.

He is bolder, even to the point of reckless. When we were kids I would watch how he got into fights or into trouble with teachers, and I'd decide to take a safer path. He still acts, I watch. Bicycling around Europe in his midsixties, he had an accident and fell off his bike and was taken to a hospital, where he received several stitches. After he'd phoned from abroad, asking me to pick him up at the airport and drive him home, I waited for him at the receiving entrance, and he had a dazed look, a bandage on his head, glancing around and not recognizing me at first. It was disturbing to see my older brother so vulnerable, so mortal; yet it gave me pleasure to be entrusted, as the younger sibling, with his care.

When we were teenagers, people would cruelly tell him I was the better-looking. Now, he is the more handsome. He has retained a full head of hair, while I have lost mine, following our father's tendency to baldness. He usually wears a full beard and has a commanding stare (no longer hidden by spectacles, thanks to laser surgery).

One of the ways we differ most is that my brother identifies with our mother, and I with our father. Both our parents have died, but they continue to rule our psyches and orient our moral compasses. Our mother was a flamboyant, lusty, histrionic personality, for whom the term *larger than life* could apply. She had wanted to sing and act, was thwarted for many years by having to work and raise a family, but in the last decades of her life she did perform onstage, acted in TV commercials, sang in supper clubs. Our father was a withdrawn, self-taught intellectual who wanted to be a writer; he lived what Matthew Arnold called 'the buried life', toiling as a factory worker and textile clerk. He was the taciturn scapegoat of our family: my mother divorced him in old age and placed him in a nursing home. While they lived together they made an odd couple: Eros and Thanatos. I felt sorry for my father; our fates became permanently entwined when I assumed his literary ambition, not entirely to his pleasure, since it meant both honoring and replacing him. My brother, on the other hand, never got along with our father and retains very little fondness for him. Lenny drew his strength from the example of my mother, who threw herself, with bravado, into the fray as an entertainer.

When we were younger, my brother wanted to be an artist. As a child he painted battleships and self-portraits; he was an excellent draftsman. Inclined always to the more austere, rigorous artists, such as Piero della Francesca and Roger van der Weyden, in his twenties he graduated to abstraction, studying at the university with such luminaries as Ad Reinhardt and Mark Rothko. His paintings tended in a geometric, color-field direction. They were good, I thought. Had he continued, he would certainly have made a go of it.

But he claimed he was dissuaded when he saw others doing the same sort of painting as his, only better; he thought he lacked the requisite passion to devote his life to painting.

Each of the four Lopate siblings has had artistic ambitions: my brother wanted to be a painter; I, a writer; Betty Ann, a musician; my youngest sister, Joan, a filmmaker. As it turned out, I was the only one who successfully cobbled a career out of my art. This fact looms large in my mind, and fills me with a dark mix of gloating and survivor's guilt. (I said we were competitive.) Regardless of the greater adulation my brother receives, or the argument that radio might be construed as his art form, I continue to feel I hold an edge, based on the idea that my writings have at least a chance of enduring, while his improvised radio chatter disappears into the ether. His is a journalist's way of knowing, facts gathered for the day and ejected once the occasion is over; my writing process, I tell myself, is a deeper, more arduous intellectual pursuit.

One of my greatest flaws is the need to regard myself as superior to those around me, and to position myself in such a way that they will feel it, too. Knowing full well that there are many different kinds of intelligence and that, besides, we are all ultimately dust and atoms under the aspect of eternity, I persist in wanting to view myself as the most intelligent person in social situations. That exaggerated self-regard undoubtedly colors my relationship with my brother in unhelpful ways. I insist on holding the 'wisdom' and 'maturity' cards, and on considering myself the more 'reflective'. But he overlooks it, perhaps because he is finally the more ample-spirited.

Together we look forward to sharing all the pleasures of old age: nostalgia, illness, incontinence, senility, abandonment. We will not abandon each other, I hope, because the world is less lonely for me as long as my brother is in it. He has been, if not the most important relationship in my life, certainly one of the most defining. I have made it a point alternately to be like him or not to: either way, he has been my lodestar. I'll say more: he has been my personal metaphor for Life itself, in all its encompassing, onrushing urgency.

# – Wife or Sister? –

## ABRAHAM AND SARAH IN EGYPT AND GERAR

A border incident. Abraham, like many travelers, is worried about being stopped and detained by customs guards for bringing something problematic into the country – in this case, the beauty of his wife. So he passes off Sarah as his sister, to save his own life, and she is brought to Pharaoh as a playmate, and Pharaoh, well-pleased with her, rewards her 'brother' with wealth. Then God intervenes and Sarah is given back to her rightful husband. A scandalous story, one of the most unnerving in the Bible: even if you do not consider Abraham 'ignoble' (the word Harold Bloom uses), at the very least he seems dishonest. Later, Abraham repeats the ruse in Gerar, and this time Sarah becomes the consort of King Abimelech.* (The scenario is repeated a third time in Genesis, when copycat son Isaac palms off Rebecca as his sister to this same, incorrigibly gullible Abimelech.)

Taken together, these three episodes are referred

* The first episode, in Egypt, occurs before Abram's name has been changed to Abraham, and Sarai's to Sarah; the second incident, in Gerar, takes place after the name change. For convenience's sake, I will refer to the couple throughout this essay as Abraham and Sarah.

to by scholars as 'the wife-sister stories'. I am no biblical scholar, but the stories intrigue me. My plan for this essay is, first, to examine the ways that experts – rabbis, folklorists, anthropologists, literary critics – have written about the wife-sister narratives; then, to consider the psychological viewpoints of Sigmund Freud and Karen Horney on incest, intimacy, and marriage; and, finally, to tell an episode from my own past which I associate, rightly or wrongly, with the Bible tales. I hope to line up all three perspectives like images in a stereopticon, superimposing one over the other over the other to produce a more three-dimensional sense of quandariness.

## 1 ABRAHAM AND SARAH

Rabbinical commentators have labored to put a positive spin on Abraham's deceptions. The customary approach in the Middle Ages was to vilify the other nations as barbarians, accentuating their bloodthirsty and lecherous tendencies, thereby justifying Abraham's fears. These commentators were not above racism, as when one elucidating legend, or *midrash*, has Abraham warn Sarah, '"now we are about to enter a country whose inhabitants are black-skinned, and therefore your beauty will be all the more conspicuous." Compared to Sarah's beauty, all other women were as monkeys.'* The

* *The Midrash Says*, selected by Rabbi Moshe Weissman.

contrasting modern tendency is to downplay the husband's apprehensions, as when Harold Bloom writes that Abraham 'oddly fears that his wife's beauty will expose him to danger' – the word oddly making him sound almost paranoid.

One classic *midrash* imagines Abraham going much further to protect Sarah than the terse account in Genesis. In this version, the tax collectors ask Abraham about the contents of his casket, and Abraham answers: barley. No, it must be wheat, they say. Okay, I'll pay the tax on wheat, answers Abraham. The exchange keeps escalating, until he volunteers to pay the taxes for precious jewels and gold, at which point they demand the casket be opened, and they see the ravishing Sarah.

Not all the classic rabbis exonerate Abraham, however. The great Ramban (Nachmanides) unequivocally says: 'Know that Abraham our father unintentionally committed a great sin by bringing his righteous wife to a stumbling-block of sin on account of his fear for his life. He should have trusted that G-d would save him and his wife and all his belongings for G-d surely has the power to help and save.'

Somewhere between Ramban and the vindicators lies the analysis of Radak (in Nahum Sarna's paraphrase)

> that Abram was confronted with a moral dilemma, forced to make a choice between two evils. If he discloses the truth he

> will be killed, and his wife, beautiful and unprotected in an alien society of low morality, will assuredly be condemned to a life of shame and abuse. If, however, he resorts to subterfuge, she may be violated by some Egyptian, but at least husband and wife would both survive. It would have been improper, then, to have relied on a miracle as an excuse for inaction.

Even if we grant Radak's defense, why the need to repeat the story? Surely, if a patriarch's actions look dubious the first time around, our uneasiness can only increase when the story is told twice more. The formalist, literary-critical answer is that reiteration was a 'desirable and characteristic feature of the epic tradition' (Sarna). We are still left with fitting this strange piece of behavior into Abraham's overall biography.

Let us take a closer look at our protagonist. A nonconformist, Godhaunted man, he leaves the safety of his home at a word from the Deity, wanders like a 'discontent' (Bloom's term) here and there, temporarily relinquishes his wife by pretending she is his sister, shows reluctance to send away his second wife, Hagar, makes land deals and grows wealthy, unsuccessfully tries to stop God from destroying Sodom, yet comes close to sacrificing his own beloved son Isaac because God told him to, grieves when his wife Sarah dies, and remarries (according to one *midrash*, going back to Hagar). Vacillating one moment, zealously rigid the next, cowardly and brave, the quintessential father figure (as his name change from Abram to Abraham indicates) who nevertheless takes eighty years to sire a child, he merits our sympathy precisely because of his inconsistencies.

It is tempting to compare Abraham to Odysseus. Both are wily survivors, but it is hard to imagine Odysseus hiding behind a woman, or loaning Penelope to a foreign potentate. Odysseus is a man of action and physical prowess, the classic hero, whereas Abraham is 'aheroic' and 'belongs to the paradigm of the fool' (to use Peter Pitzele's terms). Still, as Pitzele notes in *Our Fathers' Wells*, Abraham is a visionary, with a power of spiritual obedience and inward listening which Odysseus utterly lacks. Odysseus would never wander the globe at so vague an instigation as the call of God. And nothing Odysseus does is as noble as Abraham's expostulating with God to save the people of Sodom, trying to bargain the Almighty Himself into compassion.

The folklorists see the wife-sister stories as variants of popular tales about the hero's beautiful wife who risks being kidnapped by a rival prince, and who proves faithful or unfaithful (Helen of Troy, for instance) in the process. One difference between the Greek epics and Genesis, however, is that often the Bible characters are made to appear less heroic, the better to demonstrate God's power. It is God alone, not her husband, who can protect Sarah, by inflicting plagues and boils (read: sexual dysfunction) on Pharaoh, and by sewing up the wombs of the Gerarites so that no one in the land can get pregnant, much less Sarah.

The wife-sister stories also allow the biblical authors to crow about the beauty of the Jewish matriarch (all the more remarkable when you consider that she is well past eighty!). I like the *midrash* that says Abraham was so discreet (or unobservant) he had never before observed how lovely Sarah was. But, says Ramban, 'Wading through a stream, he saw the reflection of her beauty in the water,' which has the delicacy of a Japanese haiku. After which, he became Sarah's booking agent, you might say.

When Pharaoh, after being afflicted by God to prevent intercourse, bombards Abraham with rhetorical questions ('What is this you have done to me! Why did you not tell me that she was your wife? Why did you say, "She is my sister," so that I took her as my wife?'), the patriarch makes no reply. A modern reader might think Pharaoh has a point. He acted in good faith, showing generosity toward this sojourner; it seems unjust for God to punish the Egyptians when Abraham misled them. Later, in the story's Gerar reprise, King Abimelech addresses Abraham in wounded tones similar to Pharaoh's: '"What have you done to us? What wrong have I done that you should bring so great a guilt upon me and my kingdom? You have done to me things that ought not to be done. What, then," Abimelech demanded of Abraham, "was your purpose in doing this thing?"'

It is worth wondering what the biblical authors had in mind by putting such rhetorically persuasive passages into the mouths of the heathens. Abimelech's questions are too direct to be avoided; this time Abraham must speak up, and he does. Source analysts, in fact, argue that one of the reasons the E writer repeats the story that J has already written is precisely to give Abraham a chance to defend himself the second time. The E writer's variant also takes much greater pains to show that Sarah's virtue was untainted – that Abimelech never got a chance to sleep with her – while the earlier, Egyptian episode by the J writer had been less reassuring on that score. In *The Book of J*, Harold Bloom sees such distinctions as proof that J was the more terse, irreverent storyteller ('J has no particular affection for her patriarchs'), while E is 'characteristically . . . prissier'.

The only problem with this reading is that Abraham comes off looking worse, in some ways, in the Gerar episode by E than in the Egyptian episode. The first time he may be excused by fear; the second time begins to look like cynical realpolitik. Abraham's motivation in going to Gerar was initially weaker, argues Devora Steinmetz in *From Father to Son*: this time there was no famine, and Abraham was putting more at stake the second time by letting Sarah become another man's wife. Since God had already promised Sarah she would become pregnant soon, the paternity of the heir and the whole bloodline might be compromised.

Moreover, Abraham's spoken defense, when it finally comes, is not that impressive. As Devora

Steinmetz observes: 'He . . . gives more than one explanation, which suggests that no one explanation was good enough.' In fact, he gives three explanations: (1) 'I thought . . . surely there is no fear of God in this place, and they will kill me because of my wife.' We have no way of knowing how reasonable was this apprehension, but we do know that Abimelech demonstrates plenty of fear of God, after the Deity comes to him in a dream and warns him not to touch Sarah. (2) Next, Abraham utters this surprising statement: 'And besides, she is in truth my sister, my father's daughter though not my mother's, and she became my wife.' No previous genealogies in Genesis suggest so close a kinship between Abraham and Sarah. Either he is improvising a yarn, which would make him a liar, or he is telling the truth that she is his half sister, which would convict him of incest. Some rabbinical commentators believe that he is merely throwing sand in the heathen ruler's eyes. Modern apologists for Abraham have argued that because the Israelites were 'underdogs', they had a right to practice deception, as part of a 'trickster' culture. Somehow, mendacity justified by minority status does not entirely sit right.

Suppose that Abraham is telling the truth and Sarah is his half sister. One anthropological explanation has it that while incest was certainly taboo in Abraham's day, the prohibition may not have held as strongly between half siblings. There is also the argument advanced by Ephraim Speiser (based on some

Nuzi tablet fragments), that Abraham was only following a common practice borrowed from the neighboring Hurrians, to 'marry a girl and adopt her at the same time as his sister'. Adin Steinsaltz, the renowned Talmudist, takes a similar approach to Speiser in his book *Biblical Images*: 'Moreover sister was a common term of endearment for a woman in early Eastern culture; for instance, in the Song of Songs, we find "My sister, my spouse" (5:1) and "My sister, my love." . . . The sister-wife as the chief wife, as opposed to the other, secondary wives who were "outsider".'

I find this whole line of thought interesting but beside the point. The story's power lies precisely in the fact that Abraham is frightened for his life, and so he asks Sarah to pretend they are brother and sister. If Abraham is not lying when he asks Sarah to do so, but is merely using an honorific, the story loses its guilty tension and is reduced to a lexical misunderstanding. Devora Steinmetz puts it perfectly: 'Even if, as some have suggested, Abraham's claim refers to a specific type of aristocratic marriage . . . Sarah is still Abraham's wife, and Abimelech is not free to take her.' I also like Ramban's commentary: 'Even if it were true that she was his sister and his wife, nevertheless when they wanted to take her as a wife and he told them, She is my sister, in order to lead them astray, he already committed a sin towards them by bringing upon them a *great sin*, and it no longer mattered at all whether the thing was true or false!'

Which brings us to Abraham's final excuse: (3) 'So when God made me wander from my father's house, I said to her, "Let his be the kindness that you shall do me: whatever place we come to, say there of me: He is my brother."' If the first part of Abraham's statement suggests an attempt to shift the blame onto God, the second part gets to the crux of the matter: he admits that not only did this deception occur in Egypt and Gerar but it was their regular arrangement. They were like scam artists using the same brother-sister masquerade in each town.

What of Sarah's feelings in all this? Ilona Rashkow, in her feminist critique, *The Phallacy of Genesis*, views the wife-sister story cycle as a paradigm of 'powerful male/powerless female/uninvited sex'. She points to Sarah's 'silence' as evidence of her being treated as chattel (although elsewhere, I must say, Sarah has no problem opening her mouth: she objects loudly to her rival Hagar's presence, and scoffs at God's promise that she will conceive). Rashkow, not unreasonably, indicts the biblical tale as sexist: 'The irony is that Pharaoh, Abimelech, and I as a reader understand the immorality of adultery, and the crime of female sexual sacrifice, more readily than Abraham.'

Adin Steinsaltz sees it very differently, reading into Sarah's silence a noble, group-oriented spirit:

This silence did not arise from passivity or surrender, nor from a wish to be taken by another man, nor because Sarah was a mere tool of her husband: her acquiescence was obviously prearranged with Abraham, with whom she worked as a team on the basis of decisions jointly made. Here, they had decided, despite the shame and humiliation involved, that it was preferable to preserve the wholeness of Abraham's camp – representing, as it did, the new ideal – even at the cost of Sarah's honor. This willingness to sacrifice her personal well-being for the common cause is surely borne out by the fact that Sarah never reproached Abraham for the injury done to her; nor, indeed, did she even mention it.

To Steinsaltz, we may take Sarah's silence for consent; to Rashkow, the opposite. There is no end to the moral interpretations we can extract from these Bible stories, which is why they are so invaluable. I am not in the business of judging Abraham or Sarah. What interests me is the fluid way this couple kept crossing the line between spouse and sibling, and what that might indicate in a larger sense about the situation of marriage.

## 2 SIGMUND AND KAREN

The first time I registered the story of Abraham passing off Sarah as his sister, I felt a shiver of recognition. I could identify with Abraham's faintheartedness, since I am not that physically brave a man myself, and might resort to any number of pusillanimous strategies to save my neck. But there was more to the shock of familiarity, something more personal, as though I had once done the same thing but could not remember when. It was the same sensation as when I've dreamed that I'd already killed a man, or already married my mother or slept with my sister, and now, the next morning, must sort out the aftermath of that abomination.

I thought of a passage I'd read in Karen Horney's provocative essay 'The Problem of the Monogamous Ideal'. One of the reasons people marry, wrote Horney, is to fulfill

> all the old desires arising out of the Oedipal situation in childhood. But the increasing intimacy within marriage leads to a resuscitation of the old incest prohibition – this time in relation to the marriage partner, and the more complete the fulfillment of unconscious wishes, the greater is the danger. The revival of the incest prohibition in marriage is apparently very typical and leads *mutatis mutandis* to the same results as in the relation between child and parent; that is, the direct sexual aims give place to an affectionate attitude in which the sexual aim is inhibited.

The way I'd read this passage was this: even, or especially, in good marriages, where the partners communicate well, there is a tendency to begin as lovers and end up as brother and sister.

Now, perhaps Horney's formulation will seem merely a psychoanalytic restatement of the age-old folk wisdom that marriage is the surest way to kill off sexual passion. The Talmud also tell us: 'Since the destruction of the Temple, sexual pleasure has been taken away from those who practice it lawfully and given to sinners, as it is written: "Stolen waters are sweet, and bread eaten in secret is pleasant."' What Horney contributes to this sour truism is an explanation: that the decrease of sexual pleasure in marriage comes about not merely by habit but because of a revival of the incest prohibition. It is almost as though one were revirginated by intimacy, which carried within itself the stigma of familial trespass.

Although the incest taboo projected onto the spouse could well be Oedipal, I chose to see it in the light of siblings – wives being rounded into sisters, husbands into brothers. Most likely, this exclusively 'sibling' reading of the Horney passage came from the fact that I grew up with two sisters, both younger than I, both very attractive; and each could not help but figure into my erotic imagination. Both my sisters are slender, brunette, and about five foot five, which matches a type I have consistently fallen for. So for me to say that the wife becomes a sister figure is by no means to rob her of a sexual dimension. One difference between the conjugal tie and the brother-sister tie may be that the latter, because unconsummated, never loses its erotic edge.

While parsing what she calls 'the affectional attitude in which the sexual aim is inhibited,' Horney acknowledges her debt to a well-known paper by Freud, entitled 'The Most Prevalent Form of Degradation in Erotic Life', in which he analyzes the tendency of some men (usually of the bourgeoisie) to suffer a polarized split between affection and sexual desire. 'Where such men love they have no desire and where they desire they cannot love,' declared Freud. Inhibited by the incest taboo, and overesteeming their mothers and sisters, they can only be potent 'when the sexual object fulfills the condition of being degraded', either because the woman comes from a lower class or because she has loose morals. Just as important, she 'does not know the rest of his life and cannot criticize him' for 'perverse' sexual longings. 'It is to such a woman that he prefers to devote his sexual potency, even when all the tenderness in him belongs to a higher type.'

The modern middle-class male may not have as much Victorian propriety to rebel against, or as developed a courtesan demimonde to turn to, but much of what Freud says holds true, else why the need for the Playboy Channel? He concludes with a sharp, audacious assertion: 'Whoever is to be really free and happy in love must have overcome his deference for women and come to terms with the idea of incest with mother or sister.'

Coincidentally, Freud refers to Genesis in this essay: 'A man shall leave father and mother – according to Biblical precept – and cleave to his wife.'

Now, to return to our wife-sister story: Sarah is the mother figure in Genesis, the Matriarch of Israel. Moreover, she is getting on in years – close to ninety, so the text tells us; even if we consider the figure an exaggeration and halve it, she has definitely entered her matronly period. Somehow the shadow of 'mother incest' will have to be lifted or diffused for the marriage to revive. Curiously, Sarah is also barren: her greatest anguish is that she is not a mother. She urges on Abraham her servant girl, Hagar, and with this 'less exalted sexual object', as Freud would put it, he regains his potency – i.e., fathers a child. This, in turn, awakens Sarah's jealousy and her power as a woman.

They have, in a sense, an open marriage: just as Sarah tempts Abraham into infidelity by giving him Hagar, so Abraham hands over his wife to strangers. That their marriage has lost some of its oomph and needs replenishment is suggested by the episode when Sarah laughs scornfully at the promise of childbirth. She does not expect her old codger of a husband to be able to pleasure her. (There is a wonderful commentary on this in the Babylonian Talmud, which Francine Klagsbrun quotes in her *Voices of Wisdom*:

In the book of Genesis, when God tells Sarah she is to have a son, she laughs and says, 'Now that I am withered, am I to have enjoyment – with my husband so old?' When God relates the incident to Abraham, He is recorded as saying, 'Shall I in truth bear a child, old as I am?' According to the rabbis, God deliberately changed Sarah's words in telling them to Abraham so as not to reveal that his wife had complained of his old age. At the school of Rabbi Ishmael it was taught: Great is the cause of peace, seeing that for the sake of peace even the Holy One, blessed be He, deviated from the truth and modified a statement.

It seems odd that, at the moment Abraham awakens erotically to his wife's comeliness, he desexualizes her by assigning her the role of sister. But perhaps they are keeping the sexual roots of their marriage alive by playing these taboo roles: you be the sister, I'll be the brother. One could argue, following Freud, that Abraham reinvests Sarah with even more sexual interest by placing her in a compromising situation, where she becomes the potential plaything of other men, thereby whetting his jealousy.

In another essay, 'A Special Type of Object Choice Made by Men', Freud wrote that with certain men

> a virtuous and reputable woman never possesses the charm required to exalt her to an object of love; this attraction is exercised only by one who is more or less sexually discredited, where fidelity and loyalty admit of some doubt . . . Not until they [these men] have some occasion for jealousy does their passion reach its height and the woman acquire her full value to them.

You might say that Abraham forces this most faithful of wives to play the role of a courtesan, a light woman, as a means of recharging the marital spark. By the way, I am not seriously maintaining that this is what happened: for all I know, there may never have been a historical Abraham. I am only suggesting that these undercurrents, when examined, make the story come alive more for me.

Let me turn by comparison to a modern variant of the wife-sister story: Paul Bowles's *The Sheltering Sky*. In this novel, Port and Kit have been married for twelve years and have evolved into a sort of brother-sister pair. ('"Like two children," he thought, "who aren't allowed to go on a picnic with the family."') They have long since stopped making love, but they are dependent on each other, and Kit feels convinced that Port could not be interested in any other woman. Actually, he has sex with an Arab prostitute, a 'degraded sexual object', in Freud's terminology, unbeknownst to Kit. Port is a wanderer, like Abraham, and he, too, places his wife in danger, by inviting along a very handsome acquaintance of theirs, Tunner. But he rationalizes that she is faithful ('What the hell, he'll never get her'). Actually, Kit does end up sleeping with Tunner. Port is also afraid, like Abraham, of the alien culture through which they are traveling, and this fear motivates a good deal of his behavior: '"I wonder if after all I'm a coward?" he thought. Fear spoke; he listened and let it persuade – the classical procedure.' Port also places Kit (and himself) in danger unthinkingly by traveling to a place without adequate medical facilities, and then falling gravely ill. After he dies, she is ravished by Bedouins and lets herself become their sexual prisoner.

Port and Kit represent the nightmarish turn that might have happened to Abraham and Sarah without God's intervention. As it is, the biblical duo suffers a multitude of troubles – barrenness, separation, wife-mistress tensions, brother-in-law problems – and yet somehow they hold together as a couple. To what extent has their ability to modulate into siblings, as a sort of protective coloration, facilitated this conjugal longevity? Maybe they are only following in the footsteps of their ancestors, for were not Adam and Eve also brother and sister, in a sense, coming as they did from the same parentage?

## 3 PHILLIP AND CAROL

I was married for the first time at twenty; my wife, Carol, was twenty-two, but the two-year difference seemed utterly negligible, or if anything, desirable, so eager was I to catch up with everything older than I. We both felt mature for our age, and our marriage was a way of signaling to the world our eagerness to take on the responsibilities of adulthood. In retrospect, I see I'd grossly overestimated my maturity; I was only bluffing, miming the part of a grown-up.

Shortly after our wedding and my graduation from college (Carol had already been out in 'the real world' awhile), we cashed in our wedding presents for a year abroad. We took a Yugoslav freighter, then the cheapest way to cross the Atlantic. I remember the chess-playing, goatish Yugoslav sailors trying to get me drunk on slivovitz so they could make time with Carol. But I had confidence in her loyalty. I had married her not only because she was so brainy and attractive (a sandy-haired anthropology major interested in writing fiction, with sparkling green eyes, a cute figure, and a rueful smile) but because she was so sweetly responsive and dedicated to me. Though I was not surprised to see that many men, like these sailors, were attracted to her, it did not make me particularly jealous because, in the dynamic of our marriage, I was the one treated as the peacock, the visionary, and she, the devotee. She was the daughter of a Viennese psychoanalyst and had been trained to honor men who presumed to think. I was the son of textile workers who had been trained to venerate Viennese psychoanalysts and their progeny.

The freighter touched down in Tangier, where we spent a fascinating week (Arab culture carried for us, as Jews, excitement, fear, and something archaic, ur-Semitic) before traveling on to our real destination, Spain. During the next ten months, we settled into a nesting routine: both of us wrote fiction while we lived on the tightest of budgets. To give ourselves one final treat before flying back to the States, we decided to return to Morocco for a month of tourism. Spain had proven somewhat disappointing – too much like America, perhaps – but Morocco had seemed genuinely different or, as we say now, Other.

Carol was the perfect traveling companion: good-humored, curious about everything, willing to match my stride mile for mile. As we walked, we would compare observations and dissect characters we had met on the road. We enjoyed imagining that we thought as much alike as any two people could, and part of our conversation was devoted to ensuring that accord (even if it meant my not noticing the degree to which she was yielding her own position to my more dogmatically asserted one). Young couples traveling often like to fantasize that their thoughts and feelings are in harmony, that they hold no secrets from each other – that they are two halves of the same psyche. Perhaps it comes from the anxiety of journeying into a threatening world: the 'Orphans of the Storm' syndrome. We were two young people somewhat frightened of life, and we clung to each other like brother and sister. I've seen many graduate student couples take on that sibling quality, gladly sacrificing youth's sexiness for the comforts of a more stoop-shouldered, reasonable companionship. At least temporarily: sometimes they wake up five years later and decide they've missed out on the Zeitgeist, the sexual revolution of the moment. That is more or less what happened to us. But even after I'd kicked against the constrictions of having married too young, I would often think: if only I'd met her when we were both older, in our sixties, say, we could have been the happiest pair, the perfect middle-aged couple, traveling in retirement, going to museums, comparing impressions after dinner parties.

In any event, there we were in Morocco, on our way from Marrakech to the next big city, Casablanca, which would be our last stop before taking the plane back to New York. We had boarded a bus for a ride that began at dawn and was scheduled to last twelve to fifteen hours. I don't know what Moroccan buses are like now, but in 1965 the roads were primitive, the bus driver inexperienced if not new on the job, and each mountain curve he took threatened to plunge us into the ravine below. I also had a throbbing headache and a nauseous, carsick feeling – probably occasioned by the couscous I had eaten in the marketplace the night before, though Carol seemed to be showing no ill effects from it. My only consolation was that the bus would be stopping for an hour in a hill town called Béni Mellal, roughly at the midway point of the journey.

Béni Mellal was a town that seemed to exist solely for the purpose of letting travelers stretch their legs. It may have also been a trading and agricultural center, but what I noticed chiefly on deboarding were the beggar kids with hands outstretched, the teenagers offering or threatening to take your luggage, the flies, the chewing gum vendors – all of which might have struck me as diverting on another day, but with the hard-boiled egg I'd gobbled at dawn still squatting on my chest, and my bowels making ominous pincer movements, I felt an urgent need to sit down and close my eyes. The Moroccan heat and sun seemed especially oppressive, and there was no shade in sight.

'What's wrong?' Carol asked. I told her I needed a john fast and was not sure I was fit to continue. If Béni Mellal had an inn of some sort, it might be good to spend the night there, and catch another bus to Casablanca tomorrow.

We were in luck: Béni Mellal had a more than adequate, even pleasant hotel at the top of the hill, run by ex-colonials. It was an obstinately Parisian oasis, with onion soup at lunch and French sports papers arriving six weeks late.

After visiting the w.c., I took a nap, and Carol went to reconnoiter the town. An hour later she returned to say that Béni Mellal was more interesting than it had at first appeared. With her anthropologist's training, she was always scrutinizing hill towns on our travels, with an eye to what sort of study she might do if she had a grant and a year or two to stay put there. This time she had met a man on her walk who told her that that very night Béni Mellal was to host a Moroccan music festival. There would be folk music scattered throughout the village. 'What a shame you feel so rotten!' she said. 'Oh well, maybe you'll recover in a few hours and we can both go out and hear music. Everyone says it's going to be great.'

I was too sick to care. My plans were to stay close to the toilet: if Blind Lemon Jefferson or Leroy Carr had risen from the grave to sing at the local hall, I would have passed him up. 'You can go if you want to,' I assured her. Actually, I wanted her to stay back and take care of me, and I even half-assumed she would, as she was usually such a good nurse in those situations. But she surprised me by accepting my offer. She may have said, 'Are you sure it's okay for me to go?' but by this time I was too locked into my noble-martyr pose to abandon it. I did not like to seem one of those boorish husbands restricting their wives' fun. It was a test: I wanted her to choose to stay at my side, without my asking her to. Always a mistake to say the opposite of what you mean. So she left.

I began shivering in bed, unable to get warm, and the insides of my stomach swirled until I thought it might be a good idea to vomit, and from that thought came the instant realization that I could not *not* vomit, which I did with my head over the bowl. I felt like a child again, unable to control my involuntary reflexes. A run of diarrhea followed that lasted for several hours. A maid came in to mop up the excess vomit on the floor. She helped me back to my bed, asking: 'Where is your wife?' Where, indeed.

It was ten or eleven at night before I could finally stop running to the bathroom. My mood had shifted, from self-pity at being abandoned to worry about Carol: Why hadn't she come home yet? What if something bad had happened to her? I waited a quarter hour more, then got dressed to look for her. I was not in the best shape to go searching, but I had no choice. I needed to go out into the Moroccan night, into a strange, pitchblack town I knew not at all, and – protect my wife.

I headed down the hill toward some music that was issuing out of a square white shack. I had made up my mind to signal from the doorway, if she was inside: she could get up, apologizing to her guide, and we would walk home together, not without a lecture from me. Or maybe I would skip the lecture. I opened the door and saw fifty men sitting in burnooses and embroidered caps, with hashish pipes at their feet. No sign of Carol. I forced my eyes to move row by row over the dark faces, in case I had overlooked her. The eyes that met mine were imperturbably grave, telling me I had no business intruding on their ceremony. The plangent, trancelike, bluesy music, a cousin to Coltrane, appealed to me deeply, but I was not there to play the concertgoer. I moved on.

In the distant hills, I saw scattered cottages with lights on, and moved toward each, backtracking across the town in this way for the next hour. I passed more than once the all-night café where truckers sat hunched over stools, passed the bus stop where poor Moroccan women patiently waited with string-tied parcels, passed the boarded-up market stalls. Each time I entered a music hut I would see men crouched on the floor, listening stolidly to the instrumentalists. There were no women in these audiences. What could Carol have been thinking?

Around 1:00 a.m. I met a sympathetic-looking young man in a djellaba, who asked me in French whether I needed help. I replied in French that I was looking for my wife, she had gone to hear some music. He insisted on accompanying me and, with that persistent hospitality toward lost strangers one encounters abroad, never left my side. I was glad for the company, but not for the way he kept questioning me: 'Why is your wife not with you?'

'She wanted to hear the music.'

'And you were sick? And she left you?' He shook his head: incomprehensible. Proof that the decadent West no longer had any values. Even more incomprehensible was that I had entrusted my wife to a man whose last name I didn't even know.

He stopped by his fiancée's house to tell her what he was up to, and she, a spirited young woman from what I could make out through her veil, joined us. Though they conversed freely, she walked a step or two behind him. I could not have been given a sharper demonstration of the proper respect a woman in that part of the world is expected to show her man. Not that I had any desire to embrace a reactionary, chauvinistic system that kept women in chador, but I was ashamed of myself for not having been able, in this place, to look and behave more like their idea of a man. It now felt cowardly on my part to have let Carol take off by herself, not only because I really wanted her to stay behind with me when I wasn't feeling well but because I had put her at risk by letting her go. For the sake of appearing liberal-minded, I had made her subject to God knows what dangers. I promised God and myself I would never do that again, if only she would materialize at the next corner.

By two-thirty in the morning we were ready to try the police. We decided to check back at the hotel one more time. I was overjoyed to discover from the hotel clerk that my wife had returned. I could not thank the young Moroccan couple enough; they, for their part, were happy that everything had turned out well, and tactfully left without insisting on meeting her.

In the room Carol seemed chastened. Reluctant to talk. She said that the man and his friend had driven her to the outskirts of town, ostensibly to hear music. They were obsessed with American movies, Doris Day movies in particular. They had obviously cast her in a Doris Day mold, which made them avid and resentful. They craved everything they saw in these movies, the Frigidaires, the swimming pools. They tried to rape her, but she managed to fend them off and make her way back into town. I held her: she clearly needed comforting; the lecture would have to wait.

We stayed for five days longer in Béni Mellal, while I regained my health. During that time I tried to learn, without much success, a little more about what had happened to Carol that night. While I took her word for it that she had not been raped – I think she would have been more distraught if she had – a part of me continued to wonder if more had happened than she was letting on. In any case, our two minds no longer seemed utterly in sync. How had it happened? I kept brooding. How had I so misjudged her? She had always seemed the most reliable, prudent woman imaginable: perhaps because she was two years older than I, I had projected onto her a maternal–big sister solicitude. What I had failed to notice was that she was still a young woman herself, struggling to sort out her desires, a side of her probably resisting the 'good wife' role. On the other hand, maybe I was making too much of it: what had she done after all that was so culpable, except to exercise some poor judgment?

Béni Mellal produced the first fracture of trust between us. I had an urge to get revenge. In time to come there would be other infractions, mutual betrayals. I pondered my own complicity, using the memory of Béni Mellal to worry feelings of unmanliness. Had I been too much a brother with her, not enough a husband? Was I what Hemingway called an 'American boy-man', a Francis Macomber? Had I tempted her into neglecting me, to satisfy some atavistic scenario of disappointment?

Freud teaches that every love object is but a surrogate for the original one, and must disappoint because of that. Had I known what I know now, I might still be married to Carol. No, scratch that. Abraham and Sarah could forgive each other again and again for their ambiguous adventures; but perhaps that's the difference between an older man's wisdom and a younger man's bluff at intelligence. 'All things can be replaced,' says the Talmud, 'except the wife of one's youth.'

# – The Limits of Empathy –

I am thinking a lot about empathy these days – defensively, I might add – because my wife keeps accusing me of lacking this quality in relation to her. Of course, I readily agree. I sympathize with Cheryl's pain but stop short of empathizing with it. My saying this infuriates her even more, and she is the kind of person who has no shyness about retaliating. Her retaliation makes me even more disinclined to oblige. I explain that what feeble mechanism I might have for empathy is nullified when I'm being attacked: I cannot identify with a person who wishes to cut me to ribbons. That is my imaginative limitation.

At what point, I wonder, did the word *empathy* begin to displace sympathy? *Empathy* isn't even in my 1971 *Oxford English Dictionary*, which may reflect the more reserved character of the British: one assumes the rage for empathy began on this side of the Atlantic. (See Bill Clinton's famous assertion, 'I feel your pain.') A recent edition of *The American Heritage Dictionary* tells us that while sympathy 'denotes the act or capacity for sharing in the sorrows or troubles of another', empathy 'is a vicarious identification with and understanding of another's situations, feelings, and motives'.

To me, *sympathy* suggests a humane concern for others' positions or plights, based partly on a general ethic of compassion for all living things. *Empathy* conveys, to my mind, a stickier, more ghoulish shadowing that stems from the delusion that one can actually take on oneself, or fuse with, another's feelings.

It is possible that my wife wants to recapture that sense of romantic communion we had at the beginning, which is usually strongest during the infatuation phase, when lovers' hearts are said to beat as one. But I can't help suspecting she got this empathy bug after a few sessions with her therapist, Barry.

Since then, as a result of our frequent bickering and my wife's conviction that her therapist is a marvelous human being, we have entered into couples counseling with Barry. To my surprise, he is a marvelous human being. Wise, reasonable, scrupulously evenhanded, and empathic – perhaps to a fault. Sometimes, when he commiserates about the pressures we are operating under – raising a three-year-old with health problems while juggling our careers – I begin to wonder about this warm compassion, the depth of which, it seems to me, should be reserved for Romanian coal miners, not yuppies like us.

In one session, we were recounting a disagreement we had had the night before. As it happened, about sex. We had been going through a dry spell, mostly because of my wife's preoccupations with our baby daughter and her mistrust of my capacity to empathize with her.

Now she said she was getting ready to consider doing it again, and I replied, like an idiot, something to the effect that I'll believe it when I see it.

Barry offered an alternative script, giving us the lines that, in his view, we might more profitably have spoken. I was to compliment her on making this overture to an advance, and if I still needed to express skepticism, she was to show that she understood my 'vulnerability' because I'd been starved for sexual affection. Barry then asked what I thought would have happened if she had replied that way. Feeling the old obligation to speak the truth in therapy, I took a deep breath and said that his suggestions had nothing to do with life as it is lived, that he was trying to indoctrinate us into the new, totalitarian Empathy Speak.

'Are you really against empathy?' he asked, somewhat incredulously.

'I am, yes –'

'You see?' said my wife. 'You see what I have to put up with?'

I went on to say that I was for sympathy, that old-fashioned term. The people I admire most, like two friends of mine both in their seventies, operate out of a moral code older than empathy that acknowledges that the gap between two souls can never be entirely bridged. I thought of my old professor Lionel Trilling, who questioned in class D. H. Lawrence's hunger for total honesty in a love relationship by saying: 'Why should two people have no secrets from each other?'

On the other hand, there is much in the present culture that promotes an exaggerated or false sympathy, like the figure of the talk-show host, the Great Listener, Oprah or Geraldo, whom I consider spurious.

As you might imagine, this did not go over well. I saw that my attempts to explain myself were perceived as inappropriately 'academic', therefore cold, therefore removed from emotions and the business at hand. (Interesting: that therapy today has that anti-intellectual quality. This is no place to start *thinking*.)

When people start speaking of reason as a 'defense', I get nervous, considering where the irrational has gotten us in the last hundred years. And, grateful as I am for Barry's willingness to help straighten out our problems, I can't help watching my tongue now in counseling sessions. I have a lingering suspicion that many couples therapists train you to say not what you genuinely feel but what is less confrontational, all the while telling you that they want you to be in touch with your feelings. No, they want you to make nice.

I suspect I will never be able to empathize with the panic and depression my wife sometimes feels – for the simple reason that they both terrify me too much. I grew up far too close to such emotions in my parents, and it took all my strength to distance myself from their debilitating pull so as to form a workable, reasonably cheerful self. Where does that leave the marriage? My wife still hungers for a more empathetic soul mate, while I am equally convinced that I am realistically offering something else that is of value. Call it an understanding of limits, based on the intractability of human nature and the intensely problematic – not to say tragic – dilemma of modern marriage.

Given my empathy-challenged nature, I am faced with the choice of trying to fake an empathy orgasm – a distasteful proposition – or waiting out my wife's rage, hoping that in the end she will come to accept my defects, as I hope and pray to accept hers. Forbearance, resignation, and stoicism still seem to me the only way to go. Someone (Buffon or Goethe?) once said, 'Genius is a long patience.' I don't know about genius, but I would maintain that marriage certainly is – at least when you're committed to making the marriage last.

# – The Lake of Suffering –

About a week and a half after my baby daughter, Lily, was born, she began to throw up. Usually a gentle gush of whitish stuff would flow down her chin, and a minute later she would seem peaceful, no worse than before. Sometimes, however, the vomiting was harsher. Since Cheryl was breast-feeding Lily, she wondered whether something was wrong with her technique (the angle of tilt, the pillow arrangement) or with the consistency of her milk.

We had been told that all babies 'spit up'. Part of our problem was that, Lily being our first child, we did not know how to distinguish between normal postnatal events and symptoms that should indeed alarm us. For instance, we rushed Lily to our amiable neighborhood pediatrician, Dr Rhonda, because blood seemed to be collecting in the umbilical area. It turned out this was a natural result of the umbilical plug falling out. Or when Lily got the hiccups (another benign occurrence), Cheryl had me read aloud all the 'hiccups' entries in the child-care manuals on our nightstand, to see what we could do to stop it. (Nothing.) As the books' entries did not alter when left unattended, I didn't see why I needed to read every word aloud each time Lily started hiccuping, but doing so was indicative of how everything that first week made us nervous.

We had amassed a shelf full of baby books in the time between the start of Cheryl's pregnancy and Lily's arrival. My intellectualized response to any unknown situation is to buy a book; and since Cheryl designs books for a living, she also finds security in them. So we immersed ourselves in Dr Spock, Penelope Leach, and the What to Expect series, among others.

I could write a whole essay about these infant-care books as a peculiar literary subcategory, the antithesis of the horror genre. Suffice to say that a butterscotch of reassurance covers them: they address new parents as a set of middle-class worrywarts, counseling you that your fears are natural, even your ambivalences are natural (Leach goes so far as to empathize with the husband who resents ceding oral monopoly of his wife's breast), but that underneath, you have nothing to worry about. Spinal taps, chronic illness, oncology, and death are not listed in their indexes. They are addressed to well-baby care. As soon as the reality sank in that we had an ill baby on our hands, we closed these volumes, never to consult them again.

—

But I am getting ahead of myself. Before plunging into the story of that first cruel year in the hospital, I need to pause and consider why we had so wanted a child.

During my first marriage, my wife, Carol, and I were in our twenties, young and poor and ambitious to become writers and in no hurry to take on parental responsibilities. Our fertility seemed more a curse than a blessing, necessitating as it did two abortions. By the second abortion, the marriage was already tottering. I left it to embark on twenty-one years of bachelorhood. However staunch my political support may be for abortion rights, I eventually began to regret the two chances for fathering I had personally let slip up and to feel, at times keenly, the absence of those children who might have been mine. This feeling was accentuated by ten years of working with schoolkids from kindergarten to sixth grade, teaching them writing, theater, and filmmaking. I had stumbled into the teaching profession as a way to support my own writing habit. Not expecting to be good with kids, to my surprise I seemed to be, enjoying their odd, unpredictable ways, and I drew on these experiences for my book *Being with Children*. When parents came to pick up their kids after school, I'd gush about how much fun I'd had with their Johnny or Jill during the day, and they would invariably say, 'Yeah, that's because you don't have to take care of them after three o'clock.' I wasn't sure that was true: their remarks became a challenge I was eager to accept. I certainly liked being around children, listening in on their chatter and keeping up with their quirky behaviors. Why wouldn't I respond fairly well to my own?

By my late thirties, I was sold on having a child. The problem was I first had to find a wife. By no means had I worked through the neurotic patterns of mistrust, hostility, and abandonment that my mother and father had passed down to us as masculine-feminine relations. So I continued to stumble from one woman to the next until, at forty-seven, I met Cheryl. Widowed young, she had a deep understanding of what matters. She was formerly a painter and now an award-winning book designer, creative, intelligent, irresistibly attractive, humane, kind, and thirty-four. That last point was important: I wanted a wife of childbearing age.

Everything else seemed to be in place. I had established myself as a writer, had a full professorship at a local university, and felt an expansive willingness to take on this new work of bringing up baby. To be honest, my professional life had gone somewhat on automatic pilot: I could no longer be motivated by fear of failure, as in my younger years; I had written eight books, taught for over twenty years, and anticipated more of the same. I wanted something else, some new adventure to engross me – a child.

My wife was at first hesitant. She worried about what might happen to her career; she feared, legitimately, that much of the burden of child rearing would fall on her, and that she might get lost in the process. Moreover, having been widowed the first time and wanting to make sure the new relationship would survive, she preferred to spend our first years of married life together, just as a couple. A reasonable request, I thought. I could wait. Not indefinitely, but . . . When she had asked, before the wedding, 'What if I never want to have children? Would you still want to marry me?' I had swallowed hard, and said yes, though in the back of my mind I'd gambled that she would come around eventually.

Which she did. A few years into the marriage, she told me she was ready. She hoped to get pregnant in time for my fiftieth birthday party, giving me what she knew I wanted most in the world. As soon as she made up her mind, her eagerness for a child outstripped my own. It took us nine months to conceive – not long as these things go, but long enough to plunge us into high anxiety. Two months after I turned fifty, we received the happy news that Cheryl was pregnant, and on September 16, 1994, she gave birth to Lily.

That first week home with the baby, the shock of eighteen hours in the delivery room and an episiotomy fresh in our minds, we had no chance to catch our breaths before jumping onto the roller coaster. I am well aware that every new parent feels overwhelmed. How much of the initial hysteria would have occurred anyway, even in optimal conditions? This is another form of the question that would later haunt us: What would the experience of parenting have been like if nothing had gone wrong?

Already, by the end of the first week, Cheryl seemed a confident and placid mother. Twelve days into our parenthood, Lily began vomiting. We took her to Dr Rhonda to be weighed, and found she had lost over a pound since birth. 'Failure to thrive', those creepy, accusing words, were spoken for the first time, but only as a distant possibility. Dr Rhonda thought it might be gastroesophageal reflux; a fan of alternative medicine, she recommended trying chamomile tea, which an Andean tribe fed their babies to calm their stomachs. She also had us supplement breast-feeding with a soy formula twice a day, and Pedialyte, to prevent dehydration.

So I began feeding a bottle to Lily. Cheryl was critical of my first efforts: 'I can't believe how tensely you're holding her!' she would say, or 'Talk to her – no, not in that dead monotone voice!' I'm sure my technique left much to be desired, but it seemed to me adequate to the purpose; underneath Cheryl's criticisms was the real fear that, unless we fed Lily in a letter-perfect manner, she would vomit. (As we later learned, she was regurgitating not because of something so preventable as the wrong bottle angle but because her system couldn't process protein correctly, a far more serious problem.)

One Saturday, toward the end of the second week, I offered to watch the baby while Cheryl made herself breakfast. After giving Lily a feeding, I held her upright for about forty minutes, as I had been instructed, then let her sleep on the bed. Lily was napping peacefully, when suddenly she woke up and began choking. She turned bright red. I lifted her in my arms to get her upright, but she arched her head rigidly away – choking, spewing, gasping for breath. It was the most frightening thing I'd ever seen. She's going to die, I thought, right in front of me, and I can't do anything. I was also terrified that this was a seizure and began thinking epilepsy, brain damage. 'Cheryl,' I yelled. I placed my hand under Lily's head for support but was amazed at the strength of her arching away. Cheryl ran up the stairs and entered the room shouting, 'Don't let her arch back so, that's the worst thing in the world, she'll choke on her own vomit!' I started to explain that I'd been trying to support her head, but she cut me off, shouting, 'You're killing my baby!' I completely understood her accusatory panic, but could not stop myself from feebly defending my child-caring skills. A part of me was prepared to believe that I *had* caused the whole problem, and shrank back, letting Cheryl take over. But the attack seemed to have an involuntary dynamic all its own. (Later, the doctors confirmed that head arching during projectile vomiting is a reflex in some infants: nothing you can do but let it run its course.)

In retrospect, that red, choking baby reminded me of the creature from *Alien*. I wonder how much horror imagery comes from our terror of the crying newborn. The theory that Mary Shelley wrote *Frankenstein* after losing her baby makes sense to me.

I called Dr Rhonda, but she was away all weekend. In desperation I phoned Dr Lou Monti, a pediatrician connected to Mount Sinai Hospital, where Lily had been delivered. He suggested we take her off the breast milk and soy and give her nothing but Pedialyte, and if she couldn't hold that down, to bring her into the hospital for observation. Lily threw up the Pedialyte; we drove to Mount Sinai, turning her over – with relief, I confess – to the high-tech medical team of pediatric gastroenterologists led by Dr Neal LeLeiko. Dr Monti was retained as Lily's pediatrician. Dr Rhonda, with her holistic, soothing chamomile, was off the case.

—

The initial diagnosis at Mount Sinai was that Lily had a severe milk-soy allergy. Perhaps the little bit of soy-based formula we had fed her (it only takes a drop) had led to the stripping of her intestinal villi, the hairy coating that aids digestion. The analogy the doctors used was it was making a carpet into linoleum. I believe Lily's physical problem or condition was in place before any of this happened, but giving her the soy milk formula was like feeding her poison.

It is not easy for an unscientific layman like myself to explain, even now, the exact nature of her medical problem – especially since it baffled all her doctors for so long. In the first two years of Lily's life, a good deal of effort was spent in eliminating the possibility that she had some known condition (which, however dire, they would have known how to treat), such as pyloric stenosis, cystic fibrosis, lympathic dysfunction, Crohn's disease, or some autoimmune disorder. They never really did come up with a clear diagnosis: the closest one was 'protein-losing enteropathy', a vague way of saying that she had a gastrointestinal problem with the transport and absorption of protein. This would cause some of the protein she ingested to 'spill' into her bloodstream, instead of being absorbed by her cells as nutrition. Testing the blood for albumin was the only way to measure the degree of protein absorption in the body. We began to live or die by two numbers: Lily's weight and her albumin level.

As soon as Lily was admitted to the hospital, my wife made a remarkably heroic and, I think, correct decision, that one of us would stay with the baby at all times. This meant, as it turned out, that Cheryl spent a few years off and on in the hospital, putting her own professional life on hold, though she still managed, amazingly, in retrospect, to produce freelance book designs for Soho Press from the hospital room. She would sleep (or try to, in the interruptive nocturne of clinics) on an army-style cot next to Lily's crib. Some nights I or my mother-in-law, Doris, would spell her. But for the most part Cheryl was there, to see that the erratic night staff did not make a mistake with Lily's meds or the machinery. (It happened once that a night nurse was about to administer meds intended for a different patient when Cheryl caught it and stopped her.) Just as important was the guarantee that Lily would receive as much stimulation as possible, keeping her mentally sharp. We had seen some ward babies, left to the check-and-run care of nurses and attendants, who would stare listlessly up at the ceiling for hours or keep wailing until someone had a moment to look in on them. Cheryl's vigilance paid off for Lily, though the sleep deprivation, worry, and fear took a toll on her, leaving her exhausted and despairing.

If the arrival of children routinely places a couple under pressure, nothing can put more stress on a marriage than a child's illness or life-threatening disease. In our case, each of us had a different way of handling stress. Cheryl's took the form of mastering all the physical procedures involved with Lily's care, so that she could assist and, in effect, stand in for the night nurse. She became so adept that she probably could have passed a nursing examination – and the nurses would often let her do their jobs. But she got furious with any bungling: a tigress protecting her cub, she would throw nurses out of the room if they were about to make a mistake, or dismiss interns if they took too long finding a vein to draw Lily's blood, or forbid anyone, even surgeons, from approaching the crib without washing their hands first. She was not afraid of antagonizing the staff.

My way of facing the crisis was to stay stoically calm, pleasant, diplomatic, offending no one in authority; to remain upbeat and hopeful. I also tried to play the supportive husband, though whenever Cheryl's anxiety led her to lace irritably into me, I withdrew a good deal of my support. But mostly I struggled just to hang on.

Before Lily's hospitalization, I'd had my share of childhood traumas, betrayals, unhappy love affairs, and deaths of friends. But in a sense I'd led a charmed life, in that I always felt strong enough for the circumstances that presented themselves. In fact, I had often felt stronger than my circumstances, fantasizing a reserve tank of energy and courage that I might tap into if, suddenly, I found myself in a grueling or dangerous situation. Faced with the experience of Lily's illness, I quickly went through my reserve tank. My Superman fantasies were ended. I was discovering the irregular nature of courage: two days of heroic pluck, two days of blank despair. Besides, our heroism seemed beside the point; what was needed was patience, a different, more demanding virtue. Now we were In It. I understood what it meant to suffer, really suffer, night and day: to be up to our necks in the lake of suffering.

—

I was commuting in a triangle between Hofstra (my teaching job at the time) on Long Island, Mount Sinai Hospital on the Upper East Side of Manhattan, and our home in Brooklyn, where I fed the cats, looked at the mail, and crashed. Often I would drive to Mount Sinai directly from work, taking the Long Island Expressway to the Midtown Tunnel, then driving up the FDR Drive to Ninety-Sixth Street, relinquishing any residue of work solace and professorial dignity the closer I approached the hospital.

The neighborhood around Mount Sinai, how well I came to know it! Those sad take-out delis, those bleak bagel sandwich places, the bar and grill restaurants, the florist shop, the five-story tenements with fire escapes along Madison Avenue, the vertical parking garage, the whole borderline gestalt. It seemed fitting that Mount Sinai nestled in a no-man's-land between the posh apartment buildings below Ninety- Sixth Street and the East Harlem public housing projects, which started above 100th Street, because as soon as I entered the hospital complex, I had the feeling that I was nowhere, in a liminal no-time zone along with all the other marked creatures, crawling past the soda machines in the underground tunnels that connected the various wings and pavilions, a whole planet of illness, a leper colony. I would take the elevator up to the fourth floor (Friday nights and Saturdays, to honor the Sabbath, it stopped automatically on every floor), making way for the gurneys in the elevator, and prepare to hold my breath for six, seven, eight hours. The hospital was like a spaceship: no gravity, no up or down, white, weightless.

After you had spent a time-crawling morning and afternoon etherized with small talk, inedible meals, and diaper changes, putting up with the painted clowns, social workers, and clergy who came by on their mercy missions to the children's ward, checking out the art therapy–storytelling room for the twentieth time, the doctor would arrive around four, on his rounds, and everyone would snap to attention: the day would acquire a shape, good or bad, depending on the words he let drop or his tone of voice.

A hundred years ago, a baby with Lily's condition would likely have died. Then came the invention of the Broviac catheter: a device surgically attached to a main artery, which transmitted a slow, steady stream of nutrients to the bloodstream, bypassing the digestive tract entirely. With a catheter inside her, Lily would gain weight regardless; it was like riding an escalator, up up and up. No more anxiety about failure to thrive. The catheter was a godsend, but it had a tendency to become infected at the entry site after a while, and when that happened it had to be removed and another artery found. (The body has a limited number of arteries for this purpose, a scary thought when considering the future.) Catheters also require a sterile environment, extensive tubing, and a semistationary pump that has to be monitored regularly, making a patient less portable, and a baby more awkward to hold.

Cumbersome and daunting as this was, we also disliked the less surgically invasive nasogastric tube, which went down Lily's nose. Not only did it mar the perfection of her face and give her skin rashes, but it required a nasty insertion procedure: you had to stick a thin NG tube down her nostril and keep pushing until it came to rest in her stomach, all the while with her flailing, screaming, and twisting her head to avoid that unpleasant gagging sensation. She soon figured out how to yank the tube out of her nose: flick a fingernail under the surgical tape and rip it loose, triumphantly. Then we would have to hold her down, ignoring her wails, and reinsert it.

The hospital universe preoccupied us. Though I still craved the outside world, it began to recede in reality and color, partly as a consequence of our isolation: no one on the outside knew what we were going through, and we couldn't explain it to them. I would get home some nights and find messages on the answering machine from friends and relatives: 'Tell us what's happening, we can't stand the suspense.' They wanted to hear that everything was all right. It wasn't. Some people still didn't know about Lily's illness and would leave messages saying: 'Congratulations! You must be on Cloud Nine!' I would try to get through all these calls as speedily as possible. Cheryl had designated me the one to stay in touch with and debrief our circle of friends and relatives. But after several such conversations, relaying the same information, I felt awful.

I began to suspect people's motives (idle curiosity? Schadenfreude?). Sometimes little things that were said seemed so insensitive: a friend bragging about how much her child was eating, another forever mentioning news items about medical breakthroughs that had nothing to do with Lily's illness, or telling some anecdote about a second cousin who was born with stomach problems and now played tackle for his high school football team; another saying that if we just fed Lily mashed bananas, all would be well. Yet I knew if they didn't call, I would also have felt slighted. I came to realize that there was nothing anyone on the outside could say or do that would be right. The only person I could talk to without feeling wounded was my friend Max, who had a little girl with problems even more severe than Lily's: her disabilities had resulted from a botched delivery, and now she could not speak, or walk, or eat without assistance. When she was first born, I thought their situation unimaginably pitiable. Now we shared the same vocabulary: Broviac catheters, endoscopies, Mic-Keys . . . Max was my reality check. He told me that, when it first happened, he refused to talk on the phone and hated everyone. Now he just hated most people.

Friends and relatives, unable to grasp the nature of Lily's difficulty, wanted me to go over and over the details, which I hated to do. When her problems didn't get solved with dispatch, they told me to change doctors, though we knew we had the best. Lily's chief physician, Dr LeLeiko, is one of the top men in pediatric gastroenterology, a brilliant analyst of the facts and a humane, wise practitioner, a cultivated savant such as one might encounter in a Balzac novel. He listened to my exasperation with the outside world and said: 'The problem is a social one. In America, babies are not supposed to be sick. If they're sick, people expect one of two outcomes: one, the baby dies; two, she gets all better. Americans don't know how to deal with chronic illness.'

—

Of course, Lily was not just a medical rarity but an increasingly defined, plucky little person whom you couldn't help but fall in love with – a charmer, who 'lured people in', as one doctor put it. First (I say this as a completely unbiased father), she was the most startlingly beautiful baby, with porcelain skin, flashing dark eyes, long eyelashes, masses of black hair, cupid lips. 'Like a porcelain doll,' everyone said, and her mother dressed her in outfits accentuating that old-fashioned Victorian look. Second, she had remarkable interpersonal skills: from the moment her eyes could focus, she would fix you with an interested gaze, follow you around the room, react with pleasure or laughter if any opportunity offered, allow herself to be held and hugged by visitors, and generally flatter them with her attention. It is conceivable that babies or small children who undergo, like Lily, the pain of needles, splints, CT scans, and spinal taps, may develop survival skills that enable them to mature faster in order to attract the love of adults. Lily was the pet, the darling of the ward: sometimes she would be brought up to the nursing station, catheter pump and all, and hang out amid the residents and nurses as they were having conferences, ordering meds or take-out food, answering the phones. Her three male physicians competed for her love. The best attendants on the floor – Aloma and Averill from the West Indies, and Norma from Chile – were all devoted to Lily: bathed her, changed her, sang to her, helped her stand, encouraged her to take her first steps around the crib. One hospital study, I was told, confirmed that babies perceived as 'cute' received more care than those seen as homely. Lily's beauty and winning ways seemed at times a Lamarckian compensation.

—

In March, Lily looked healthier, and there was talk about going home in a few weeks. Then the lab test came back, showing her albumin level had plummeted to 2.1 (3.0 or above was considered healthy). No one knew the reason for this setback: maybe they were pushing her too fast, maybe it was a lab error.

I remember vividly an occasion around that time when, to cheer us up, one of the best nurses, Suzanne, came in with two gifts: pearl earrings for Cheryl, and a tape of Disney's *The Lion King*, which had just gone on sale that day. Suzanne wheeled the fourth floor's VCR and TV into our room so that Cheryl, Lily, and I could watch the movie in bed. (Cheryl had this specific hopeful vision that we would all be home someday, nestling on the bed together like three little bears.) *The Lion King* opens with scenes of rejoicing over a newborn, which struck us with bittersweet poignancy. I dozed through the middle: I was so tired those days that I would nod out as soon as you put me in front of a TV. Lily and Cheryl napped, too. When the film was over, Lily seemed restless, so Cheryl decided to feed her. I prepared the bottle. Lily was crying and agitated as the bottle approached. I thought, Something's wrong, let's not do this. But we went ahead anyway, because we felt it important to keep up the habit of oral feeding, in preparation for that day when Lily would be taken off catheters or gastric tubes. Cheryl brought the bottle to Lily's lips, and Lily puked up everything, all over her mother's blouse. For mesmerizing spectacle, there was still nothing like Lily throwing up: I was frozen in watcher mode. 'Get some cloth diapers, get a wet washcloth, do something!' cried Cheryl. I bustled about, trying not to gag from the sour milk smell of her formula vomited up, and castigating myself: Why didn't I say anything? Warn her not to feed Lily? Well, Cheryl was the one in charge, I rationalized, I didn't feel I had the authority. But we were always looking to blame each other for Lily's vomiting, as though it were simply a matter of human error. Would that it had been.

Shortly after the *Lion King* episode, we agreed to Dr LeLeiko's recommendation that we suspend oral feedings. LeLeiko wanted to regulate strictly the quantities Lily was receiving and did not like these random extra feeds; he also feared that they might exacerbate Lily's reflex tendency to vomit, since liquid was being introduced from the bottle at a faster rate than drips through the tube. Cheryl had been resisting his advice, afraid, as it turned out rightly, that, if we suspended bottle feedings, it might be more difficult to get Lily to take food through her mouth later on. Perhaps something else was behind her resistance: she felt bad enough that she could no longer breast-feed Lily; at least she could give her a bottle from time to time and fulfill some of the maternal role of feeding her baby. But we acceded in the end to the doctor's request: no more oral feedings, for the time being.

Seven months into this ordeal, we wanted desperately to get Lily released from the hospital: that became our main focus. For one thing, she did not seem as sick as many children on the ward, some of whom had leukemia or equally serious diseases. One boy, the child of Hasidic parents, passed away, then a little Hispanic girl, and we did not want to have to witness any more deaths. In plain English, we had had it with the hospital; however kind the staff had been, we wanted out. Lily kept catching colds and getting infections, which set back her progress. In a children's hospital, you pick up every retrovirus and infectious bug. Then she started to do well; her albumin level had even risen up to 4. We had battled with the insurance company for months and finally got it to agree that we were entitled to night nursing if and when we went home. (Since Lily was still on a Broviac catheter, she would require constant nursing care during her nocturnal feeds.) Finally the word came down: we could leave. The nursing staff threw us a going-away party, we drank champagne with funny hats on, packed up the room, and said good-bye to Mount Sinai.

I was surprised that Cheryl did not seem happier.

Here, a difference between our characters, or between fathers and mothers, asserted itself. As soon as I ascertained that Lily was not in mortal danger, I breathed a huge sigh of relief, whereas Cheryl continued to be distraught because there was still no clear explanation of what was wrong with her baby. Feeding a child is so basic a part of a mother's functioning that she could not sit still and wait for some far-off improvement. 'Will this kid ever eat normally?' she kept worrying. She fretted if Lily's bowel movements started becoming looser, and was as attentive to her stools as the old soothsayers to Pharaoh's. She worried if Lily's skin looked blotchy. At the time I thought her pessimistic, but now I must admit it was Cheryl's acute maternal observation that made her quickly pick up danger signals. Two weeks after we came home, she voiced what I had been thinking but dared not say: that Lily was starting to look puffy. The medical term was edematous, an indication of not absorbing protein well. 'I'll bet her albumin's fallen,' Cheryl predicted grimly.

'Oh, not necessarily,' I said. 'It could be just a cold.'

A month later we were back on the ward. All the symptoms had returned, one by one. Her albumin had shrunk to 1.9, which only confirmed the external signs: throwing up, diarrhea, swelling in the face and fingers, distended stomach, lethargy. Jane, the able chief nurse, and our favorite attendants – Aloma, Averill, and Norma – were sorry to see us return but helped us settle into our old room. We were living a recurring nightmare, back in the trenches. The first day on returning to the hospital, I felt a powerful desire to write the whole story of Lily's illness; the words were marching through my head, and writing seemed the only way of releasing the emotions within me. The next day I felt devastated, had no desire to write, wanted to lie in a fetal position and be fed intravenously myself.

Cheryl this time took it better than I, acted calmly, perhaps because she was at this point a pessimist. I had directed all my energy to getting out of the hospital: we'd done it, I was happy, I felt we had put the whole sorry story behind us. And then to go back inside made me crazy. I didn't know what to live for. A healthy Lily, of course. But how? Cheryl admitted to me in private that she was fighting off a major depression. She would do her weeping in the bathroom. She had just enough energy to attend to Lily and the medical professionals but not to the outside world. Seeing mothers feeding their normal children or pushing strollers in the street would scald her. She had stopped returning friends' phone calls. Other people couldn't give her what she wanted, so she had no interest in them.

'What do you want from them?' I asked.

'An answer. Make the problem go away. I know it's irrational, but I have so much anger against the world. And so much guilt, for having borne a sick child.'

'Why guilt? You've nothing to feel guilty for. That's wacky.'

'You're not a mother, you wouldn't understand. I feel guilty, that's all. And then people tell me I need distractions. I should get out more, jog around Central Park, see friends for coffee, go to a movie. What a joke! I'm not interested.'

—

More setbacks, other recoveries. A little over a year after she was born, Lily came home again. There had been fears that she might have developmental or intellectual delays, as is common with babies institutionalized the first year, but for the most part she tested on track for her age. We still requested physical and occupational therapy, so a couple of these therapists came to our house to work with her. I would usually accompany the physical therapist to the local park, where we would help Lily climb the jungle gym or go down the sliding pond. Lily began speaking early, forming complex sentences and making jokes, flashing a large vocabulary. By three years old, she was quite the chatterbox, and continued to be unusually perceptive and alert to others. At four she would engage the neighbors in long conversations. She was taken off the catheter but remained fed by a gastric tube, which was now inserted in her stomach. The line led behind her into a knapsack, which contained the pump and her formula, hidden from strangers' sight; Lily herself could forget about its existence, which meant we no longer had to guard every second against her tearing it out, as we had with the nasal tube. She got forty-five-minute feedings five times a day and for much of the time when she slept at night. The rest of the day we could take her off the feeding and she could run free, more or less, though within our anxious sight.

—

Without getting saccharine, I would like to describe at least some of the journey by which we came to a healthier, happier time.

Cheryl and I, with the invaluable aid of my mother-in-law, Doris, made an enormous effort to normalize our situation. When strangers encountered Lily for the first time, we uttered no allusion to her condition, feeling it was none of their business. The only obvious anomaly was that she was small for her age (the euphemism the household favored was 'petite'): at seven, she might be mistaken for a five-year-old, at nine for a seven-year-old. But if someone commented on her lack of height, we said nothing about her first years in and out of hospitals. I think we were ashamed, as parents often are when their children are not completely 'normal', though the way we framed it was that we simply did not want to advertise Lily's condition because it might turn her into an object of pity. A crossroads occurred when Lily had a setback in first grade, and had to miss several weeks of school during a return sojourn in the hospital. When she came home, we no longer had the option of taking her off her tube feeding all day: she needed continuous, slow-drip infusion. There was some debate in the family that she might be stigmatized if she went to school with the feeding pack in plain sight, and homeschooling was discussed as a temporary option. I decided it was more important to send her to school every day, to let her make friends and be socialized, even with the feeding pack attached. Fortunately, her classmates took it in stride and embraced her. Children at that tender age can seem blessedly tolerant.

Lily's constitution remained very fragile through ages six to ten: she still vomited too often and had diarrhea. A new symptom arose: she would sometimes get the shivers, and need hot tea and piles of blankets to arrest them. She would neither eat nor drink by mouth, though there was nothing anatomically preventing her from swallowing. It was more a psychological problem: having missed the earlier milestones, she was afraid of gagging and vomiting, and had to learn painstakingly from point zero how to eat – a seemingly natural act for a younger child. It would have been too risky a gamble to cut off her feeding and see if hunger might prompt her to learn more quickly. She was very small for her age and needed every calorie to count.

We went through a troop of feeding therapists, all of whom practiced some variant of behavioral modification. I remember one of them crooning and zooming the spoon like an airplane into (or onto) her clenched mouth. Another counseled our leaving the room, abandoning her, so to speak, if she refused a morsel. A third boasted a 100 percent success rate, but nevertheless gave up on us. Lily resisted eating by mouth for the longest time: she was not the best candidate for a rewards-and-punishment system, being stubborn and independent; and, it must be said, neither Cheryl nor I ever cottoned to behavioral modification, so perhaps she was picking up on our skepticism. Nor were we, snobs and loners that we were, willing to join the various parent support groups that might swap stories about their own children's eating struggles, or place Lily in a hospital for a month of strict supervision and tough love. Dr LeLeiko, too, was dubious about these approaches, and thought we were wasting our time.

'When she's ready to eat, she'll learn,' he said. He was increasingly sanguine that her malabsorption problems would resolve and her body learn to make adaptations. In fact that is what happened. Her organs adjusted to whatever enzyme or endocrinal imbalance might have caused this illness in the first place. I don't remember exactly how or when, but she began eating normally, with a healthy appetite and a preference for Asian cuisine. After careful monitoring indicated that she could gain weight normally through regular ingestion, my wife decided to remove the feeding tube. All this while Lily was getting taller: our goal was to see her one day reach five feet, and now, at seventeen, she stands at five foot three. She is, for all intents and purposes, a healthy teenager, which means she is snappish, moody, dictatorial, and self-absorbed; but she also has a warm sense of humor, writes poetry, acts in plays, makes beautiful ceramics, dotes on her cats, and tolerates her parents reasonably well. Mother and daughter continue to enjoy, and at times endure, a semiumbilical attachment: the more Lily's health has improved, the happier, lighter in spirit, and more easygoing Cheryl has become.

The transformation in Cheryl is equally remarkable. Lily's sturdiness gives her great satisfaction and, I hope, a deserved sense of accomplishment, since it is mostly due to her efforts and years of sacrifice. We still watch Lily microscopically whenever our only child, about to enter college, comes down with the flu, or is simply under the weather for a day – I watch with held breath for some downward spiral that, fortunately, never recurs. Fatherhood has brought me all that I had hoped. If I do not love Lily 'unconditionally' (whatever *that* means), I do love her to distraction. If because of her I was obliged to enter the Kingdom of Anxiety, such is the lot of all parents, and a small price to pay for the plenitude of her being.

Lily's illness has been the most intense, challenging experience of my life. I have my doubts that the pain I underwent taught me a valuable lesson, or made me a better person; and certainly the pain Lily underwent seems to me entirely undeserved and unnecessary. But I now know what it means to suffer – I have a set of memory images from that time that will never go away.

The curious part is that I have no desire to relinquish them: I sometimes summon these memories (such as Lily getting prepped for an endoscopy or passing under the spaceship dome of a CT scan) and fan them out like a deck of cards, just for the fright of it, just for the knowledge that that time is now past. Lily, though she writes engaging personal essays, has never written a word about her hospital time. Perhaps as a residue of our years of circling the wagons and putting up a normal façade, she sees no need to revisit those trials; she has put them behind her, like childish toys. Cheryl may have held on longer to her sense of grievance against a world that would not cut her enough slack, given the complexity of her caring for Lily, but eventually she, too, has put it to rest. It is only I – to their eyes the one who was the least involved, and hence the least entitled to claim the experience – who cannot seem to let it go. Is it because it shook me to my very core? Or is it because I am too proud of having survived that ordeal to stop dwelling on it? All I know is that a part of me continues to haunt those wards, those corridors, those nurses' stations, while seeming to attend to my ordinary daily life.

# – Memoirs of a Wishy-Washy Left-Liberal –

It is bad enough to have to read in the paper each morning some political setback to the progressive cause, some reactionary nonsense put forward to maintain unnecessary tax breaks for the rich or subsidies to the banks and oil corporations, some further protection of those who would despoil the planet. What makes it even worse is that I cannot take much pleasure in the responses of my own kind, because I know too well what they are going to say before they say it, and because there is something disagreeable to me in any political party line, which too often commits the espouser to tit-for-tat distortions and petty vituperations.

A friend phoned the other day in an outrage, because of some conservatively skewed article in *The New York Times* by a foreign correspondent whom he knew to be 'on the Right', having gone to school with the fellow. 'We have to do something about it,' my friend insisted. 'We have to counter this nauseating reactionary propaganda.' He used the word *we* with some justification, knowing that I held the same left-liberal views, more or less, that he did. But I had no intention of dashing off an angry letter to the *Times*, or whipping up a satire of the offending journalist for *The Nation*. Newspapers would always be filled with opinions that ran counter to mine, and if I were to retort to each one, I would be worn to a nub, like a fastidious fourth grader's eraser. This inaction on my part may sound like quietism or submission to the policy of 'Resist not evil', but it is more an economizing of energies, which I find myself, in middle age, increasingly obliged to do.

When I was younger, I had energy to burn. I could go on protest marches, dash off political statements, and still write poems, essays, and novellas. I didn't yet know who I was or what my limits were – I thought I might yet turn into both a writer and a cabinet minister, someone like Lamartine or Malraux or Havel. I had a slight tendency in that direction: in 1968, for instance, my peers elected me president of Alumni for a New Columbia, a left-leaning group formed during the campus strike as an alternative to the official alumni organization. We were sufficiently naïve to think that world revolution was around the corner, and that everyone who wanted to change society needed to get organized by joining some group. Alumni for a New Columbia's main tasks were to support the student strike by raising bail, providing medical assistance in the event of a police bust, and filing amicus curiae briefs in court for the arrested student leaders. It was, truth be told, a rather small organization: two hundred names on our mailing list, and a hard core of twenty working members, which included a few lawyers, a few old CP organizers from the Maritime Union who had scurried out of the woodwork, a few militant shrinks, and a bunch of writers like myself, who had graduated only a few years earlier and envied the students their rebellion. We writers tried to make the group sound larger than it was by issuing one statement after another to the press, protesting how 'shocked and appalled' we were by the university administration's 'insensitivity'.

I ended up a group spokesman, going on radio talk shows to debate the more conservative alumni or administration representative, inveighing against the university's 'complicity in racism, sexism, and the war machine'. My grasp of the facts was shallower than I would have liked, but I could be briefed quickly and was an adequate bluffer, and, besides, neither side was listening to the other anyway: it was an exercise in what a psychologist friend calls 'synchronous narcissism'. I was certainly against the Vietnam War, I liked the attention I was receiving and the challenge of thinking on my feet, but I could never get over some queasiness from indulging in strident public rhetoric which took me further and further away from my own interior musing, in which skepticism, ambivalence, and uncertainty play large parts.

I remember being interviewed once by a Pacifica-WBAI reporter in a live hookup before a campus rally. We were standing in front of Butler Library, facing the Columbia quadrangle, looking out at the lawn, and the interviewer asked me a question about strategy. As I started to frame the answer a blue jay hopped about, twittering nearby. It so mesmerized me, that bird, that I forgot to speak, and the interviewer began sweating, since nothing is more verboten to radio people than dead airtime. Finally I brought myself to utter the requisite clichés, but I couldn't forget that a part of me was truer to watching the blue jay than to caring about the impact that a new university gymnasium proposed for Morningside Park might or might not have on the adjoining Harlem community.

I was in over my head, in short. I had started reading Marx and going to classes in the SDS Liberation School, where I encountered the dazzling rigidity of left-wing sectarian thinking. It was here that I first encountered the scary slogan 'The struggle against revisionism is the struggle to the death!' It was here I first heard that we must cast out of the canon Dostoevsky ('reactionary'), Fromm and Niebuhr ('liberal'), Nabokov ('elitist'), and Hamsun and Céline ('fascists'). I had no intention of boycotting these estimable writers, and even at the time thought that grading writers by standards of political correctness was nearsighted. But I confess I was intrigued by the very sound of such clangorous, dismissive conviction.

It was here, too, I first heard human rights and civil liberties contemptuously referred to as 'bourgeois freedoms'. Could it really be said that these noble humanist ideals were nothing but a smoke screen, as

Fanon maintained, by the ruling class for domination of people of color? And could a revolutionary situation truly justify the suppression of free speech, assembly, and religion – or the mass execution of class enemies? These were chilling thoughts.

The lesson I learned most from that era was that the truth was being distorted and manipulated by both sides. Of course the United States government lied massively and daily; its misdeeds in Vietnam and neglect of our urban and rural poor were inexcusable. But we left-liberal foot soldiers were also being shamelessly deceived: told, for instance, that the People's Republic of China had no capital punishment, only re-education, as later we would be assured about Cambodia's Pol Pot that he was a good guy and don't pay attention to the lies being spread about him by the capitalist media.

Mao's China was the standard of purity, the wind from the east; Fidel Castro's Cuba, the other model held up for imitation. How well I remember a German graduate student named Fritz who had come to New York City to study what he called the 'exemplary model' of the Young Lords, a Puerto Rican ex–street gang turned political. Personally, I got a little nervous whenever the Young Lords appeared in public, with their paramilitary red berets and macho display of military discipline. This was the period when the student Left fantasized making a political alliance with street gangs like the Blackstone Rangers of Chicago – a prospect that scared the shit out of me. Maybe I saw it differently because most student radicals were disaffected middle- to upper-middle-class kids of suburban privilege, whereas I had grown up in the Brooklyn ghettos of Williamsburg and Fort Greene/Bedford-Stuyvesant, had experienced street gangs close up, and wanted no part of them.

Most exemplary of all exemplaries, of course, were the Black Panthers. That some police actions against the Panthers turned out to have been triggered by shoot-outs between rival street gangs is a part of history we on the Left still have trouble accepting. At the time, the rationalization was put forward that crimes were essentially revolutionary actions against the State. Huey Newton, who it later came out was something of a psychopathic thug, a pimp who killed prostitutes, dealt drugs, robbed warehouses – was our movement's prince and poster boy, by virtue of looking as beautiful as Paul Newman in a rattan chair while bedecked with guns; for his ambiguous, cherubic smile, even more compelling than Che's martyred scowl, we granted him all our love.

I don't mean to say that I swallowed the Black Panther rhetoric entirely back then, but I certainly felt a kinship with their 'struggle' (as we loved to say) and on one occasion even went out of the way to demonstrate my solidarity. It was during the winter of 1969, when the police were making brutal raids on Black Panther headquarters. The raids always came in the early-morning hours. Fred Hampton was shot to death in his bed during one of them, and hundreds of rounds of ammunition were traded in a Los Angeles shoot-out. Everyone I knew had the same reaction: stunned anger. A call went out to supporters to *protect the Panthers* by assembling in front of the Oakland national headquarters. The assumption seemed to be that the police would not dare to storm Panther headquarters in front of a racially integrated crowd of witnesses.

I was living in Berkeley at the time, a runaway from my early marriage, and felt that I had to 'do something'. I arrived around 10:00 p.m. at the Black Panther storefront, which was on Shattuck Avenue near the border between Oakland and Berkeley. Strangely enough, everyone who had come to demonstrate was white. We looked at each other, and our eyes snapped away in embarrassment. I could understand that no top-level Panther, no Bobby Seale or David Hilliard, had bothered to show and address the crowd of supporters, but at least they could have sent down the Minister of Fund-Raising or the Chair of the Anti-Fascist Alliance! Two black high school boys had alone been left behind the counter, to accept donations and sell the Panther newspaper; and the Berkeley ideologues, hoping to raise the teenage kids' political consciousness or at least rustle up a sympathetic discussion with them about repression, found them ill-informed. It was going to be a long night.

There was nothing to do but leaf through police

brutality literature and wait. A framed portrait of Joseph Stalin hung above the counter. Not one of my favorite leaders. *What am I doing here?* I asked myself. If the police do stage a raid, we'll all be massacred. If they don't come, we'll be disappointed.

Eventually, the group formed a 'presence' in front of the storefront, moving in a slow circle, talking about everyday matters: teaching loads, landlords. A stiff wind blew across Shattuck Avenue. Cars whizzed past on their way to the freeway without braking for a closer look. There were so many traffic lanes separating us from the other side of Shattuck that we could only make out a fuzzy pink and green of bungalows and trees across the street. Occasionally a person on foot approached us, usually a sympathizer who would be immediately pressed into our circle. If only the newcomer had not joined us but had stayed looking at us, say, from the median, our demonstration would have felt less pointless. Without an audience, we were walking in circles for the benefit of a lone streetlamp. We might as well have been protesting the coolness of the night, or the unapproachable distance of the stars.

After midnight the temperature dropped further and we tried to keep warm by walking faster or rubbing our arms. Someone went inside to make a cup of hot Postum, and brought out several additional cups for demonstrators. I was lucky enough to get one. We were suddenly in high spirits – who knows why? Maybe it was simply that the absurdity of the situation had been acknowledged and accepted. If the police *should* come, we had nothing but this hot Postum with which to arm ourselves. We must remember to throw it in their eyes.

# – Laws of Attraction –

## 1

I confess I have always been attracted to women with affectations. It scarcely matters whether the mannerism is that of a coquette or a schoolmarm, so long as she projects some theatricality. Why should artifice put me so at ease? I think because affectation implies playfulness and ironic distance from a single, integrated core of being, which promises more tolerance of my own self-mistrust. Since I don't always feel I am being authentic, or on the up-and-up, by all means let my companion be not afraid of masks. The natural, wholesome type stifles me by her solemn placidity; she seems so lacking in perverse mischief that I feel apologetically Mephistophelian beside her.

I also appreciate gestures of adornment that go beyond the natural. I like lipstick, for instance. Of course it serves no useful purpose, fades quickly, and requires constant reapplication. But it represents a festive ideal, through exaggeration, of the redness of a woman's lips. There is that suggestion that she has just eaten a cherry ice or bitten someone's skin bloody. I like the glistening sheen, the taste (if I am allowed to taste it), and the telltale evidence it leaves on the collar or cheek. It is hard for a woman to kiss you without spoiling her lipstick, but that is part of the fun. For a man of my generation, who grew up on Cyd Charisse movies, lipstick will always connote the worldly and sexy. If it has no other function than to signal that the woman wearing it has taken the trouble to prettify herself for the public, that is enough to gain my gratitude.

It seems a pity that just as I was coming into my own romantically, in the 1960s, many women started abandoning lipstick, eye shadow, and a dozen other tactics in the armamentarium of arousal. In California, where I lived for part of the sixties, I witnessed the enthronement of the no-fuss, 'natural' aesthetic. Guys would boast that their girlfriends looked much more beautiful without that gunk on their faces. The natural look seemed to be about youth: the creamy, dewy skin of a seventeen-year-old, during that optimum moment when a peachy complexion (for those lucky enough to escape acne) provides all the glow that is required. It so happens I've always been attracted to a more experienced, worn-soulful look, so I resent this privileging of youthful sincerity.

Later, cosmetics companies took to marketing 'the natural look', which required quite a lot of product, applying and then removing layers of powder, blush, eye shadow. It probably takes longer to achieve the no-makeup look than it did the older, artificial one. I agree that the no-makeup look can be very pretty; I am not fanatically antinatural. But I regard the 'natural look' as just another stylistic option.

Living as we do in a postmodern era when all historical, ethnic, and environmental styles are available to us like frozen packages in a supermarket bin, it is understandable that we contemporary Marie Antoinettes might wish to play at the pastoral, simple life. Hence the fashion in high-rise apartments for country decor, baskets and patchwork quilts and distressed furniture, everything rough-textured and naïve. Meanwhile we want our beds to be nice and comfortable, with a humidifier on the night table. Well, why not? So long as we understand that 'natural' is at best an unattainable ideal; myself, I prefer the urban, the human, and the artificial.

Art teaches us that the naturalistic effect is a cunningly arranged fabrication. Degas was fond of saying that, to draw realistically, you must distort. The natural-sounding dialogue in an Elmore Leonard story is the product of laborious sweat; actual conversation, transcribed from tapes, reads as something vague and unconvincing. When we venture into Nature, even trekking to a place with no other humans or manufactured objects, we bring our conditioned responses to the experience. We visit the Grand Canyon and see an Ansel Adams photograph. For most of us, there is no possibility of entering through the doors of perception unaffected. The natural is beyond us. We need to embrace impurity, the mixture of nature and artifice, and stop feeling guilty about it.

To return to female costume: Take the elevation of

blue jeans from a grubby if utilitarian work garment to the unaffected look in leisure wear. Blue jeans are made by petrochemical processes; so much for their naturalness. Anne Hollander, in her book *Seeing Through Clothes*, wisely summed up the contradictions: 'To justify and explain their adoption of various modes of nonfashion, women have often invoked the concept of comfort . . . Jeans worn so tight that the labia majora are clearly molded, and the wearer has to lie down to get the zipper closed, cannot exactly be called physically comfortable; it is the image of comfort that is desirable, the look of wearing something sanctioned by the fashionable ideal of comfort. Trousers are actually no more physically comfortable than skirts, with a few exceptions.'

One argument against skirts, lipstick, and other signs of stylized femininity is that they degrade a woman by turning her into an object of desire for the male gaze. While jeans may ultimately be no more comfortable than skirts, the fact that jeans are unisex means that women who wear them may feel less gender-stereotyped, less frilly, more free to act boldly in the world. On the other hand, how is it possible with a tight T-shirt and jeans to deflect the libidinous male gaze? Such a costume packages a woman's anatomy as explicitly as possible while stripping away her glamour.

I draw a distinction between glamour and physique: glamour is the allure produced by the intersection of comeliness and artifice. It requires the proper setting, good lighting, elegant clothes, and a suitable companion. It is a hard-won sophistication, not for teenagers. The ability to re-create oneself as a mystery, you would think, is an empowerment, not a diminution, of the female.

I admit that it is intensely flattering for a man to be on the receiving end of that effort. But I am willing to go to considerable bother in return, as is only fair. Nothing could be more artificial than to put on a tuxedo with button studs, cummerbund, satin bow tie. However, I have grown to like the ritual of squeezing into a monkey suit, just as I like the old-fashioned exactitude of a suit and tie. A poet I know would attend formal parties wearing a tuxedo jacket and blue jeans, to show off his independence. All he was showing was his dependence on the approval of his absent bohemian pals. Embrace formality, affectation, artifice, I say. What have you really got to lose? Besides which, the propriety of formal wear can be an aphrodisiac once you get home from the gala. There is nothing more fun than the crumpling of her gown and the wrinkling of your boiled shirt, now that sartorial perfection no longer matters. Let the dry cleaners deal with it tomorrow. Such are the joys of artifice, mixed in with a little nature.

2

Most men have certain ideal notions of femaleness derived from movies they saw in their youth. No matter how cockeyed some of these archetypes are, and no matter how manfully I struggle to assimilate the truth that women are as variable, real, and complex as men are, a part of me continues to want to match up the actual women in my life with the celluloid temptresses and saints in my imagination.

I grew up in the postwar era of dangerous brunettes and redheads, like Rita Hayworth, Yvonne De Carlo, Jane Greer, and Jean Simmons, who would no sooner look at a Robert Mitchum or a Glenn Ford than they would begin to seduce him and stab him in the back. Double-crossing came as easily to these femmes fatales as smoking a cigarette. Yet you had to sympathize with this survival tactic of what we were told was the 'weaker sex'. It was a mystery to me how this supposedly frailer sex could rise not only to a tortuously complicated duplicity but also to a level of selfless heroism that seemed outside the compass or capacity of masculine experience.

I am particularly fascinated with one convention of older melodramatic films that seems to have disappeared: the woman who stops a bullet for her man. She was usually, in classic-triangle terms, the redundant woman – say, the native mistress of a man stationed in the Orient, a rival of the newly met, supposedly more suitable white lady. The mistress is beautiful. She is faithful, she loves her man, and she has a deeper understanding of life than the white lady. So, the audience wonders restlessly, how can the hero reject her?

But because her love for her man is so deep, it transcends self-preservation, as maternal love is often alleged to do. Maybe such passionate romantic devotion exists only in the backwaters of civilization, among colonial or underworld women who have gone beyond the ladylike. Did I mention that sometimes vice takes the place of race? A gangster's moll or bar girl with a tarnished past, an Ida Lupino/Gloria Grahame type, may also administer the reproachful lesson about how far a woman's love may go for her man.

Now, just try to imagine a love so powerful that it would cause a woman to hurl herself in front of gunshots, when most of us would hit the ground. Such love no longer exists, you say; we live in a more calculating age or, to put the matter optimistically, a more progressive age, in which women are less dependent on men, less masochistic. Am I sorry to see the convention disappear? To be frank, I don't know whether to pray for such a love or to be terrified by it.

I try to imagine a man pointing a gun at me. As he starts to pull the trigger, my Chinese girlfriend blankets me with her body. She takes the bullet. As grateful as I am, I cannot help feeling there is a certain presumptuousness in someone's stealing the death that was meant for me. I am so stunned by her act that I forget to knock the gun from the killer's hands. Now he is pointing it at me again, and she has already given her life for me. Would it be cowardly to prop her in front of me, or would that be a way of honoring her original intention?

In any case, how will I shove her limp body forward at the precise moment the gun is fired? My respect for this woman is growing, not only because stopping the bullet was a noble thing to do but because it required incredible athletic timing, like a basketball player's leaping to block a shot. My own reflexes are rustier. Even if I was quick enough to stop the next two bullets with her as a shield, the gunman – always assuming he had six bullets to begin with – might get angry at the waste of ammunition. He might change his tactics, rush behind me, and shoot me in the back. How awful, to be shot in the back!

Why doesn't my other girlfriend arrive? Isn't she supposed to bring the policeman who will knock down the door and save me? All my life I have trusted in the Eternal Feminine to save me from disaster, which does not keep me in the least from suspecting all women of being betrayers. So it is inevitable that I start to think that my fiancée, my other girlfriend, may be in league with the killer. But why does she want me dead? I would have bowed out if she had asked me to. It dawns on me that she is an avenger, and that I am about to be punished for my unfaithfulness to the good mistress, she who gave her life for me.

Of course it is idiotic to expect women to die for me. The very idea must be a ghost remnant of the child's wholly unrealistic expectation that his mother will love him unconditionally, no matter how meanly he tests her or how sadly he disappoints her. And yet, when I look over at my wife playing with our orange Abyssinian cat, Newman, on the couch, I can't help wondering to what lengths she would go to protect me in a fusillade. I hope she would have the good sense to duck. I *know* she would. Nevertheless, these movie fantasies of Oriental mistresses die hard. I now begin to understand why I bought my wife, on a recent trip to China, a red silk brocade robe with dragon couchant, and why I keep pestering her to wear it.

# – Duration, or, Going Long –

Fornicating is like parenting: no matter how you do it, you have the guilty sense that somewhere other people are doing it more correctly. Myself, I wonder if I am lasting long enough. With all due attention to foreplay, penetration, and the bliss that follows, it is still usually over in half an hour, so that if my wife and I start going at it by 10:30, even with the reverential postcoital snuggle and love-you exchange, one of us still has time to say, 'You wanna watch the news?'

Of course, a marriage going on fifteen years with a little one sleeping down the hall may hardly be optimal conditions for sustaining the heights of lust. Still, I can't help wondering: if making love a half hour is pleasurable, wouldn't making love two hours be four times as pleasurable? And then there is the 'all night long' boast that Casanova and so many rhythm-and-blues singers have claimed. I have never done it all night long: with the best intentions, even in my youth, when I was more inclined to show off by going at it more than once, afterward I would feel woozily satiated, preferring to drift off or talk rather than keep banging away.

Whenever I've watched pornography, I've been

amazed at the variety and duration of these partners as they rotate front to back, top to bottom, with one orgasm after another. I take my hat off to their appetites as much as their stamina. Even knowing that filmmaking is a fragmented process, with time off for camera repositioning, I can't resist the belief that pornography constitutes the norm for humans of another, sturdier disposition. As for me, if I am stroking intently for fifteen minutes, there comes a point when I begin to think, Okay I've got the message, I've had my fun, it's time to bring this to conclusion.

What is wrong with me?

Henry Miller wrote in one novel that he kept a bowl of ice by his bedside so that he could withdraw when he felt close to ejaculation and plunge his balls into it. That strikes me as so . . . *industrious*! O. J. Simpson was widely reported to have contracted a hugely expensive coke habit in order to fuck longer. Not that either of these worthy gentlemen is my role model in other respects, but I cannot help wondering if they were onto something – if their almost puritanically conscientious focus on sexual duration may have brought them closer to a spiritual truth than I, with my laissez-faire approach.

I recently asked a few women friends what they thought of the question of duration. One woman said: 'I get bladder infections, so I really wouldn't want to be pounded for more than ten or fifteen minutes.' Good: I can do that. Another woman offered: 'Great sex tends to be quick or long. Most sex is medium-length. Obviously, most sex is not great sex.' Women characteristically say that what matters to them is the quality of connection, not longevity. In the sixties, the feminist Germaine Greer wrote that she preferred genuine passion in a male, however short-lived, to the calculated marathons that seemed to arise from performance anxiety, and that suggested the man was dulling his brain by remembering train schedules in order not to come. Indeed, though the Kama Sutra and other Eastern sex manuals stress the importance of learning to defer ejaculation for the woman's sake, it often seems that a man's desire to go long has little to do with a woman's pleasure, and more with his own competition to better his personal best.

In my own experience, sometimes when I've tried to be my partner's selfless servant in foreplay, she might say impatiently, 'I want you inside me', just as when I try to prolong the actual stroking so that she can reach orgasm first, she is apt to whisper in my ear, 'I want you to come!' Some women's orgasms are only brought on by a man's ejaculation. In other cases, I don't doubt it's because the man is not touching or stroking her sensitively enough, so she may feel: let's get this over with.

It's fair to assume that emotions affect a man's capacity to sustain himself in the sex act. But rarely is love the determining factor. First-time excitement and romantic ardor frequently shorten the act. Tenderness, from long familiarity, often results in medium-length coition. A disengaged, blasé mood may enable you to feel you can continue indefinitely. Similarly, anger: there was one lover who made me frequently enraged, whom I used to screw for a long, long time. On the other hand, unacknowledged hostility or alienation can make it difficult to keep an erection.

Clearly, Viagra and other potency-ensuring drugs have thrown a wrench into that old suspense about whether or how long you will be able to keep it up. For the very reason that they rob the sex act of one of its most interesting dimensions, anxiety, and pump up the performances of ordinary *schlubs*, who come to have a distorted idea of their amatory capacities, they should be avoided whenever possible.

I remember one woman I dated who stretched me to the limits in bed. She was a petite, pretty, rather reserved graduate student in architecture named Nina. I was teaching at the time in Houston: Nina was not my student or even in my field, but an advantage of a city like Houston is that even minor writers can acquire an aura of celebrity. Nina let it be known through mutual friends that she had a crush on me. I took her on a date and thought her winsome and very appealing in her cashmere sweater, though conversation did not exactly flow. She seemed too frightened around me to do anything more than ask an endless series of questions; I felt almost like I was being interviewed by the press.

There was no question but that we would go back to her house that first night. In bed, she lost her shyness and became the one in charge, the *metteuse-en-scène*. Everything had to be done in a certain manner. She first asked me to help put her diaphragm into her. She had very definite ideas about sexual procedure, most of which I've forgotten, except I recall that in the middle of our doing it she had me pull out, so that we could repair to the living room. There she brought me a dish of raspberry sherbet and sat on my lap. She had a wonderfully curvaceous body, and in my lap the difference between our heights (I am fairly tall) was minimized. After what seemed to her the proper amount of eating, fondling, and kissing, she let me back into her bedroom and we went at it again. Each time I showed signs of starting to come, however, she would ask me to pull out to defer ejaculation. I tried to assure her that, even if I came, I could get hard again, but she seemed not to trust that, or else somehow felt only my first ejaculation counted, and she was determined to put that off as long as possible. Hours passed this way, I increasingly baffled, though glad for the experience of having sex with a self-styled expert – until finally, rebelliously, and, I must say, more than a little bored with the old in-and-out, I let myself come. She didn't.

Which is not surprising: many women don't feel comfortable enough to have an orgasm with a man the first time. But over our next several dates, for all my efforts, hand, mouth, and member, she still didn't come. Obviously she could have orgasms and had in the past – just not with me. I remember she would vary the setups, the positions, the entr'actes. She also carefully planned a picnic, with oysters, red wine, and other aphrodisiac fare. Everything related to the art of love had a ritual character for Nina: sensuality was her religion, and she took it very seriously, even solemnly. I wondered how this shy, thirty-year-old woman from rural Louisiana had acquired such sophisticated carnal notions. It was her hidden life.

Meanwhile, we had only gotten slightly better at talking with each other, and the lack of conversational rapport added to my claustrophobic sense that the ever-stimulating, beckoning world was shrinking to this one hothouse cube of her bedroom.

I went away for the summer, to New York City, and broke up with her like a coward by mail. At the time I told myself that I had not wanted to string her along, and that it should be obvious ours was a short-term, doomed experiment in lust. Or so it seemed to me. Maybe not to her. A year later, I received a phone call from Nina, inviting me to a popular upscale cafeteria, Butera's, near the Houston art museum. I gratefully accepted. It was a beautiful day, I was on spring break. I'd been misusing my vacation, and thought how wonderful it would be to have an adventure – maybe we'd even go back to her house after lunch and make love in the afternoon.

She was already sitting at an outdoor table on the terrace when I arrived. She looked diminutive from a distance, but as I approached I saw again how voluptuous her body was. Why had I been so stupid as to break up with her? I reviewed the various reasons, the problems and incompatibilities, but still, her face looked so pretty! Especially in the sunlight, her green eyes sparkled in the most enchanting way. We selected our food and settled in. The conversation bubbled along for an hour: this time she spoke amusingly and articulately, as we both caught up with each other's lives. I took off my jacket, rolled up my sleeves – was in fact demonstrating for her a kind of projected undressing, when she looked at her watch. She said she had to return to the university library, as she was in the middle of a research project.

I felt disappointed, but intrigued: Why had she asked me to lunch? Though I could not bring myself to inquire outright, I provided a helpful silence, and she took it. She said she had called because the last time we had seen each other she had been left with an unresolved, unsettled feeling and that she 'needed a sense of closure'. I now realized that, with unintentional gallantry, I had been sitting here all this time, helping to erase myself from her troubled heart. She confessed that it had been difficult for her to make the phone call inviting me to lunch, but that it had worked out surprisingly well.

'And,' I asked, trying to keep the irony out of my voice, 'do you feel – closure?'

'Yes, I feel much better.' She went on to explain blithely that she no longer had a crush on me. Since one of our problems in the past had been her being tongue-tied, you might say she was now giving me a chance to see what a fun gal I had passed up, what a resourceful conversationalist, once her infatuated feelings for me were extinguished.

She seemed really happy to have brought off this pleasant hour. I, for my part, was burning to make love to her one more time, but was not entirely discontented to have performed my part so well. I had deactivated my charm, had provided 'closure'. I had finally gone long enough.

## – Warren Sonbert –

### FRIEND AND FILMMAKER

Until complications from AIDS claimed him in 1995 at forty-seven, the avant-garde filmmaker Warren Sonbert was the picture of robust health. Tall, with curly hair kept trim, a triangular mustache that extended from a strong nose, warm, often ironically amused eyes, and a lank, tanned physique toned from regular workouts at the gym, he looked remarkably consistent from decade to decade. Warren exuded a nonchalant, burnished vitality, and seemed never to tire, however overstuffed his schedule. He was fully present, whether at work or play (which, in his case, seemed an almost meaningless distinction, since each fed the other so relentlessly), driven by inner discipline. On the one hand the most sociable person I have ever known; on the other, by his own cheerful admission, a solitary. 'I just follow my own needs and wants and desires,' he once told an interviewer. 'Do I sound too megalomaniacal? Well, I think all artists have to be very solipsistic, very exclusive.'

I first met Warren around 1967; we were introduced by our mutual friend, Jim Stoller, who noticed Warren at a distance, leaning back in his chair in an outdoor café on Lincoln Center's plaza on a perfect summer day in June. He looked bronzed, worldlier than his eighteen years. He was wearing a brown velvet tie and a shirt with subtle tan and yellow stripes. I searched for years for such a shirt, and never found one. It's funny to think that, long before we became friends, Warren was my sartorial model on the basis of that one fleeting encounter, since, in later years, I became more of a clotheshorse, and he pared his wardrobe down to lumberjack red flannel shirts and jeans (plus the occasional tux for opera nights). In any event, I projected onto him an air of gilded youth.

Sonbert was already celebrated in underground film circles, and in Jonas Mekas's *Village Voice* column, as a post-Godard wunderkind. Curious what his films might be like, I took in a one-man screening in the basement of the Wurlitzer Building on Forty-Second Street, where Mekas's underground screenings were then held. I was very impressed. In two years, 1966 and 1967, he had made eight short films: *Amphetamine*, *Where Did Our Love Go?*, *Hall of Mirrors*, *The Tenth Legion*, *Truth Serum*, *Connection*, *The Bad and the Beautiful*, *Ted and Jessica*. They were an explosion of wry, electric imagery, each one a roller-coaster ride: you just hung on and followed.

The venerable underground filmmaker Rudy Burckhardt, himself a master of the collage-diary film, wrote about this work: 'What first attracted me to Warren Sonbert's films in the Sixties was their easy elegance of moving among beautiful people. In one scene the camera circled completely around a handsome young couple in Gramercy Park, in another fashionable models flitted by, then you could get lost deliciously in Lucas Samaras's room of mirrors. The movement seemed more sensuous and relaxed than Brakhage, and up-to-date rock music added excitement.' It was the world of sixties urban chic: boutiques and discos and art openings, Andy Warhol and Henry Geldzahler. But these fashionable subjects were not photographed as they'd been in *Vogue*. We saw both their scarlet silk blouses unbuttoned and their pimples and postnocturnal eye bags, and they were filmed in context, in their East Village apartments or on the street. His *Bad and the Beautiful* consisted of several portraits of couples edited in the camera, showing their tenderness, horsing around, relaxing with friends, clinging to each other. Someone would be lying on a bed, waiting for a lover to return from the other room. Sonbert already had the knack of creating an intensely elegiac mood about the present, as though he knew how quickly these sixties costumes and attitudes would fade. Even his Motown song choices ('Where Did Our Love Go?') accentuated the anticipated loss, as much as did the haunting tracking shots, which seemed to be searching for the separated lover.

After that first brief encounter I did not see Warren Sonbert for several years, until around 1974, when we bumped into each other, again, in the Lincoln Center area – this time at a bar after a New York Film Festival screening of Fassbinder's *Fox and His Friends*. I was with my girlfriend at the time, a poet named Kay, and I remember Warren entering with a loud group. I went up to tell him how much I had enjoyed his films, and he, in friendly response, detached himself from his entourage and sat at the table with Kay and me. He was drawn to writers, especially New York School or Language Poets. We had friends in common, and this time we hit it off immediately. I also recall Warren flirting with Kay, who was much taken with him, that night and thereafter. Kay, a Southerner, knew how to flirt with gay or bisexual men. Warren, for his part, was good at befriending both halves of a couple, and remaining loyal to each (much to my chagrin), long after they split up.

We discussed the Fassbinder film, which I (a huge fan of the German filmmaker) liked very much, and he liked less. He found its class analysis of the gay scene heavy-handed. Odd that this particular film should have been the occasion of our reunion. Kay, I think, assumed from the start that Warren was gay, whereas I tabled the question. He and I exchanged phone numbers, vowed to stay in touch, and (a New York rarity) actually did.

In the formation phase of friendship, usually one person feels he is making more of the overtures, but the advances between Warren and me seemed equally distributed. We were both men-about-town, though he was certainly more in demand; he was devoted to the punctilio of popularity, the duty not to give offense. We would meet twice a month or so for dinner, talk for hours about movies, books, work, the people we knew. I found Warren wonderfully discriminating and sympathetic. He had a way of taking your side in any dispute you recounted, while leavening his response with just enough humor to permit you to laugh at yourself.

Every time we parted, no matter how gossipy or frivolous the conversation had been, he would produce this leave-taking look, his eyes liquid from the pleasure of your company and regret at its imminent removal, his voice velvety with promise: till next time. Even if he did this with everyone, I was pleased at the effort: part of his courtly manners, from which I, who rarely modulated the abruptness of my exits, could well afford to learn.

The question of his sexual orientation did not clarify, strangely, in the first few months. For one thing, Warren never spoke, acted, or gestured effeminately; that was not his style. For another, he had the uncanny ability, like many socially gifted people, to mirror the person with whom he happened to be. Too, he may have kept back that information, leaving pronouns vague, while figuring out just how shallow or deep my homophobia ran. Perhaps *homophobia* is too strident a term: certainly in our liberal-artistic circles, it was assumed everyone was comfortable with homosexuality, and had many gay friends and acquaintances – both assumptions valid, in my case. Yet I had my moments of bitchily overgeneralizing about gays: at the very least, the novelist in me was always looking to interpret an individual's behavior as an extension of tribal or group patterns, and the gay life provided abundant material for such speculation. To give an example: once I knew that Warren was gay, I began to interpret his velvety, throaty vocal tone as the product of a constricted larynx that suddenly seemed typically gay. My thinking went something like this: gay men were often choking back considerable rage in their determination to be nice, which tightened up the vocal cords.

What complicated the issue of sexual preference was that Warren let me know, even boasted, that he'd been sleeping with a female ex-student of his at Bard, where he taught film. Though his primary sexual identity was gay, he was up for the occasional tryst with a woman, especially during this period. At the time, he seemed to be testing his sexual magnetism on everyone. According to his friends, Warren would go into a record store, say, and in less than two minutes would have made eye contact with someone, and the next thing you knew, they would both disappear into the men's room. I never saw him employ this pickup technique when he was around me, but once I realized he was gay (not from any dramatic confession: Warren was genuinely surprised I hadn't known all along), he found ways of showing me less obliquely this part of his life.

One night he took me to an all-male bash of balletomanes near Lincoln Center. It was a small apartment in a brownstone walk-up, and Warren and I got jammed behind the kitchen table with the booze. Some corpulent, red-faced queen accosted Warren with belligerent lust: 'Well, where have *you* been hiding out?' he demanded, diving into Warren's shirt and squeezing his chest. Warren took it good-naturedly, looking tolerant and amused. He was the favorite that night, discouraging no one, giving none consent. I stood by his side, for safety's sake, the only straight man there.

Later, giving Warren the opportunity to operate alone, I drifted into the living room, with its exposed brick wall. The men there, most with cropped beards, were either cruising or making out on the couch. That didn't faze me, they were not my friends, but their fierce eye contact, first intense, then hostile and dismissive when they realized I wasn't in the game, as though annoyed I was taking up space, made me uncomfortable. I felt unsure where to stand until David, a film critic and one of Warren's friends, came up to rescue me. We talked film theory: he'd been reading Noel Burch, who claimed we Westerners misread Japanese movies, we thought we grasped their core meaning, but we were being 'universalist', deceived by our bourgeois-humanist-hegemonist codes. The conversation grew more abstract the more the scene heated up around us, and for one paranoid moment I even suspected he was speaking in code, as though to say: Just as the Japanese subtexts elude you, so you misperceive the meanings here.

I kept insisting it was possible for a gaijin like me to get Ozu. The conversation went around in circles, but I clung to it, for lack of anything else, until Warren's approaching leather jacket and red flannel shirt caught my eye. He whispered, 'Had enough?' his mustache ticking my ear. I said yes, I was ready to go, and we left. Warren started laughing as soon as we hit the street. 'What an obnoxious party! Had I known what assholes would be there, I never would have wasted your time or mine.'

I was tempted to complain how alienating the whole experience had been – how straight men and gays seemed suddenly antagonists, each mocking the other's desires. But before I could deliver this harangue, I admitted to myself that the party hadn't been all that bizarre. I was exaggerating its off-putting nature to distance myself from it as much as possible. When I was a teenager at an all-male college, I had had what seemed like crushes on classmates, and worried about it. My therapist asked me: 'What are you most afraid of? The first thing that comes to mind.' I blurted out: 'Becoming a homosexual.' As it happened I didn't, and Warren did. Friends live the lives we don't have the aptitude for, or taste, or courage. What matters is that they live an alternative to one's own life.

A couple of years into our friendship Warren began dating the famous choreographer Jerome Robbins. They had an on-again-off-again relationship, and during one of the 'on' periods, Kay and I were invited to a dinner party at Robbins's town house, just the four of us. I sensed that Robbins had insufficient regard for Warren's stature in the experimental film community – that he was treating Warren like a pretty young thing and not much more; and it may have been my imagination, but I also thought Warren was showing me off that night as a friend of substance. I was determined to engage the maestro with the white Vandyke in stimulating conversation. As it happened, I had recently directed a production of West Side Story with elementary schoolchildren at P.S. 75, and I wanted to draw out Robbins's impressions of that show, which had after all been one of his greatest hits. Robbins became animated in his exchanges with me, and I – out of my dubious need to shine – flattered him with interrogative references from the forties and the fifties, which seemed to put us more on the same level, age-wise, and to exclude the other two. Warren and Kay exchanged a knowing smile, and Kay said: 'I guess we've been relegated to the wives' section.'

—

Sometime in the late seventies, after his affair with Robbins broke up, Warren moved to San Francisco, a city for which he became an avid booster. He would give *Vertigo* tours to visitors, taking them around to Ernie's and Coit Tower and other locations that had appeared in Hitchcock's masterpiece. But he would always schedule annual visits to New York, timed to coincide with his film screenings or that part of the opera season that most interested him. Over the years, Warren had become a classical music aficionado. On these fortnight visits to New York he would sometimes stay in my flat, which was small and musty but close to the Metropolitan Opera.

Warren had a curious habit of keeping a small piece of unlined white paper in his back pocket (I assume he did not use a pocket calendar because it would have made an unsightly bulge and broken the trouser line), on which he would have written his daily schedule hour by hour, from 8:00 a.m. onward. He tried to accommodate all his old friends, new acquaintances, and business associates on these whirlwind visits: breakfast with J, watching a morning rehearsal of the opera (he knew all the ushers, who sneaked him in), lunch with K, checking rushes at the film lab, then tea with L, maybe a quick movie, then a dash to the opera, after which late dinner with M, N, and O, followed by a nightcap with P and Q, . . . and perhaps after that, some catting around. On a few nights he did not return to my place at all but showed up the next morning, with an abashed 'don't ask' smile, followed by some morsels of gossip about mutual friends to throw me off the scent, then a shower and morning calls. Eavesdropping, I would hear him gathering information about the condition of the opera singers ('Tatiana has a sore throat, she may not even go on!'). Tatiana Troyanos was his then favorite: there is a lovely shot of her in one of his movies, taking a bow and receiving a bouquet. Warren was a passionate missionary for opera among his more ignorant friends. I tried to learn from him, waited in line to buy a ticket for the Paris Opera's production of *Otello*, with Margaret Price, sets by August Everding, which Warren assured me it would be unthinkable to miss. I certainly liked it, but the transcendent registers of the opera experience eluded me. I would be thrilled beyond measure for the first hour or so, then after two acts would invariably feel I'd sat long enough. But I didn't dare tell Warren that, because once, when he and I were at a *Marriage of Figaro*, before the last act some of the Met's season-ticket holders, elderly businessmen and their begowned wives, started leaving, and he hissed to me scathingly, 'Some people would walk out of heaven!'

Warren's film style had changed from the sixties: he had abandoned the Motown beat for a more severe succession of composed shots, projected absolutely silently. His suppression of the sound track had a good deal to do with his love of music, and his desire to give his visuals a 'musical' form. As he explained once in a lecture: 'In very much the same sense as one hears a series of notes, chords, or tone clusters, one sees a progression of a series of shots . . . to purely watch the images is a much freer, broader experience than any track would add. The film can truly breathe this way – go many more places than it can anchored to sound.'

This aesthetic austerity was combined with a much broader social and geographical focus. The first of his films in this manner, *Carriage Trade* (1967–1971), had an ambitious global range, and that Sonbertian knack of framing an anecdote in three seconds, but it also taxed viewers with its lengthy stream of silent images. I like what Jonas Mekas wrote about it in *The Village Voice*:

> What it is, it's a canto on people and places. It's the first canto film I know. Sonbert keeps splicing together, one bit after another (each bit about the same length, not very long and not too short) bits of footage from his journeys in Europe, Africa, India, and the United States. He cuts these pieces in such a way that places and time are completely jumbled together . . . a collage of the world, a world which seems to be the same everywhere. I don't know if there are any lessons to be learned from this film, and I have overheard some people complaining that there is nothing new in Sonbert's footage, no new information is given. Nevertheless, as I sat through these eighty minutes, I felt there was a completely different information being passed to me. . . . Something begins to happen, after ten or twenty minutes, the information is changed by time, by the ever repeating rhythms of places and people, and a new kind of information and form is born.

The eighty-minute version Mekas saw was eventually edited down to sixty-one minutes; and thereafter Warren – as though sensing that, all glories of time accretion aside, there were limits to an audience's patience – settled into a roughly half-hour format for his films. In his next, *Rude Awakening*, Warren imposed a strict conceptual grid on the editing. As he described it in an interview: 'It's very much influenced by what I would call 'directional pulls', where either the composition within the shot, or the camera movement itself, would be going either right-to-left or left-to-right . . . But I would never have a moment in *Rude Awakening* where a figurative shot would be followed by another figurative shot, or close-up followed by close-up and so on. In other words, it would be close-up, wide angle, movement vs. still, abstract vs. figurative.'

It was as though Warren were seeking the cinematic equivalent of Schoenberg's twelve-tone row. The problem is that filmed images, except for the most abstract, are not as neutral as musical notes; they cannot help but convey certain meanings, certain narrative possibilities. You watch two children playing in snowsuits in the park on-screen for three seconds and are immediately plunged back into your own childhood, while wondering about this specific pair (one seems more aggressive, the other more tentative). Depending upon how you feel about childhood (sentimental, repelled, uneasy), you project your own affective baggage onto the fleeting image. Warren was well-aware that each person 'read' his shots in a subjective manner, and even exulted in this semantic liberty: in a sense, he wanted to be the detached impresario of the spectacle, without taking a moral position himself. On the other hand, he kept being drawn to certain 'loaded' images or shot combinations, whose meaning seemed all too obvious. He flirted with cliché, only to undercut it by further shots.

To give a much-discussed example: in *Divided Loyalties*, he shows shirtless guys embracing in a Gay Pride parade, followed by a shot of a graveyard. It would, on the face of it, appear to be a sardonic commentary on the gay lifestyle. Warren was certainly not averse to taking an ironic distance from any group propaganda, including that of gays; but we also know that Warren was increasingly gay-identified from the time he moved to San Francisco, so we wonder what to make of this juxtaposition. He told an interviewer: 'Well, in one sense it may be obvious. You know, 'All is vanity.' Those beautiful bodies will eventually be dust. But what follows after that – you just can't take it from A to B without including C as well. It changes with all the things that are surrounding them. There is a shot of sheep getting clipped and another of sitting ducks on ice. It's people being exploited and not really knowing it. It's both embracing everything and being unbelievably critical at the same time.'

Formally, he is arguing for the necessity of looking at the whole film as a montage and connecting any shot to any other shot, regardless of where each falls in the sequence. Sonbert disliked Eisenstein's didactic 'dialectical' connections (shot of plutocrat, followed by shot of crowing rooster, means the rich guy is a silly braggart). But he is also a montage filmmaker, like Eisenstein: so how do you keep the audience from drawing its own simpleminded conclusions from the collision of $x + y$ images? To say that later images may complicate or contradict the simplistic equation will not keep the viewer from jumping to glib cause-and-effect conclusions based on reading two successive shots. One way Sonbert tried to evade these links was to separate two potentially narrative-making images with what he called 'palate-cleansing shots', usually of a flower or something in nature, filmed so close up as to verge on abstract. This neutral device doesn't really defuse the satiric editorial effect of other individual shots, however.

Warren was, intriguingly, a non-narrative filmmaker who loved classic Hollywood story-films (Ford, Hitchcock, Sirk, Minnelli), and whose curiosity about human behavior led him to catch people on-screen enacting tiny, three- to five-second narratives. He faced the further challenge of being an experimental filmmaker dedicated to difficulty, abstraction, and ambiguity, who also had strong political and moral points he wanted to make. He qualified his own didacticism by saying: 'Usually works are mirrors of what is contained already in the viewer, and it is the role of the creator to 'place' or qualify these reactions. Lead the viewer down one road only to diverge onto another, upset inbred expectations at the same time as exploiting these very clichés.' This sounds like having one's cake and eating it too. I wonder to what extent his desire to keep things morally ambiguous and multivalent as long as possible, his subversive urge to 'upset inbred expectations', was connected to Warren's being gay. Is it part of a gay aesthetic? Of course this subject has been worried by better theoretical minds than mine, in queer studies and elsewhere, so I risk sounding naïve by raising it. But I am trying to convey how, from a heterosexual (i.e., naïve) vantage point, one tries to puzzle out one's gay friends' inner lives, particularly if they are artists.

The paradox of Warren's films, it seems to me, is that they are both sensual and punitive, with ravishing images that add up to futility. This paradox not only is aesthetic but goes to the heart of Warren's personality. He had stunning charm and a core of anger. He may have been angry at straight society for having stigmatized him as a homosexual; he may have been angry that his mother had died early, and his father had also passed away, leaving him orphaned before he had even reached middle age. He was alone in the world – except for a million friends. The resulting bitterness or malice or urge to lash back, in contrast to his seductive, all-embracing public persona, had to emerge somewhere, and it came out, albeit masked, in his art. Note the oxymoronic, prodding nature of his titles:

*Rude Awakening, Divided Loyalties, Friendly Witness, Honor and Obey.*

He seemed quite aware of the malice latent in his film method:

> Some people are disturbed by the brevity of some of the images – particularly those that one might label 'beautiful' or 'ecstatic'. They are over before one has a chance to barely luxuriate in them, they are taken away before one can nestle and coo and cuddle in the velveteen sheen of it all, so that feelings of deprivation, expectations dissolved, even sadomasochism arise. Very often a cut occurs before an action is complete. This becomes both metaphor of frustration, hopes dashed, and yet of serenity if you like – that perhaps all of this activity has been going on, is going on, will be going on, and even all at the same time. That we are privileged viewers of many sectors of humanity.

Warren loved to have it both ways. On the one hand, admitting to a certain sadomasochistic urge to undercut expectations, pull the plug on beauty; on the other hand, expressing a desire to heal by offering us the solace of an ever-running material stream. It was in the tension between these impulses that he operated, and created a body of work that has earned him an enduring place in American experimental film.

When I visited San Francisco, I would sometimes stay with Warren, who lived just off Castro Street, in the heart of the gay district. He shared a lovely Victorian house with bay windows and a wooden stoop leading from the sidewalk to the first floor. I slept on a couch in the front parlor, which had a large piano and a theatrical arrangement of tall orange irises in a vase, and a statue of two men embracing, and a bookcase filled with *Gone with the Wind* editions and paraphernalia (his roommate was a Margaret Mitchell fanatic). Warren blithely dissociated himself from the kitsch decor, blaming it on his roommate. Solicitous of my comfort as a guest, he took me around the district the first night and pointed out which shops and bars catered to straight men as well as gays, and which I would do well to avoid – adding with a laugh that I should have no trouble picking up women. He had a mocking irreverence toward aspects of the gay lifestyle, the sartorial conformity of what he called 'Castro Street clones', for instance; at the same time he was proud of the Castro as an international attraction.

He seemed to be dating four, five, six, or seven men at the moment. One of his regulars arrived while I was reading a novel by Trollope on the back porch. I heard him go into Warren's bedroom and, twenty minutes or so later, about the length of a chapter, leave, before I got a chance to introduce myself.

Warren showed me what he called 'the playroom', a little cube-space added to the back, just above the basement. The house, located on a steep San Francisco hill, was built on stilts, and the playroom had been tucked under the back porch steps. It was the fashion, Warren explained, for many of these Victorians to have their own playrooms. This one was small, dark, with black walls, black curtains, one naked green lightbulb, a mattress with one black sheet, a Super 8 projector, and a leather harness floating in the center, suspended from the ceiling. The harness looked like some sort of torture device, though Warren assured me it was 'actually quite comfortable, or so they tell me', accompanying this statement with a strangled laugh, dismissive hand gesture, and the pleased look of a host offering a tasty tidbit to my compendium of late-twentieth-century manners.

I examined the black executioner's hood, the metal chains on the floor, and the row of shiny silver balls strung on a wire. 'What are these balls for?' I asked.

'Oh, those are from Japan. Japanese prostitutes would put them in the man's anus and pull them out one by one to induce a bigger orgasm. As I say, I never use the place myself, though we do put up guests here!' he added wickedly.

My eyes kept returning to the Super 8 projector on the night table, cocked at an angle intended to throw an image against the wall screen, and already threaded though stopped at midreel, under what circumstances one could imagine. Cinephile that I am, I was tempted to watch the film.

The playroom left a somewhat comic impression on me, like a spook house. I was not bothered by it, but I did feel threatened overall by the range of Warren's sexual activity. Not because I feared his getting AIDS – this was before we had heard that deadly acronym – but because I was repelled by that seemingly effortless promiscuity, which mocked the consequential difficulty of life as I understood it, and which felt hollow at the core, though this conclusion could have been envy. If I found in his movies an underlying emptiness, beneath the pleasure-seeking spectacle, it was partly because he put it there – describing one film as 'things not working out, things not materializing, people having certain expectations, plans, input, and those *dissolving*' – and partly because I wanted to find it there, as the apt price for his sexual freedom.

But I don't want to belabor the point: after all, I never actually saw Warren having sex, but I saw him plenty of times preoccupied with his art. When Warren was filming, usually with a spring-wound 16 mm Bolex, he did it in a relaxed, unobtrusive manner, his camera a natural extension of his bearing, like a coiled dancer's prop. Once, he came to the public school where I was working and filmed the kids and me from a gym mat, a shot that turned up in *Divided Loyalties*. When he edited there was that same blend of casualness and concentration, a toasted bagel with cream cheese lying precariously close to the slicer, on which two celluloid strips were about to be joined. Warren defied the usual precaution by cutting the original, instead of making a work print first. He relished the whole artisanal, low-tech setup of physically cutting film with a safety blade, scraping off the emulsion, applying glue, and watching the results through a flickering monitor, guided by turning the take-up reel's hand crank.

He knew there was little financial reward for his kind of filmmaking – as little as there is for writing poetry, which may explain why he felt close to poets. I used to wonder how he supported himself. The answer, I think, was partly from a trust fund his parents had left him, and partly from fees earned showing his films, partly from selling prints to archives, or occasional grants, or teaching. Within the limited remunerative constraints of his genre, he was quite successful: hustling showings, networking, cultivating friendships with festival and museum curators, both here and in Europe.

He also began writing movie reviews under the nom de plume Scottie Ferguson (the name of Jimmy Stewart's character in *Vertigo*) for a local Bay Area newspaper. These reviews were always lively, often acerbic. Gone was the gallant, omniappreciative manner of Sonbert in his youth: it had given way to a more jaundiced tone, a dislike of stupidity, as he approached middle age. Warren put it this way: 'There's so much junk around, there's so much crap. Webern talked about this – about there's so much junk, why not produce less, something really scaled down and perfected. A small, contained body, that really says it all.'

It seemed to me that Warren was making the same film over and over. He had perfected a form which suited him, and which yielded quality results, even though it did not quite express the full brio and range of its maker. I said as much in a piece I was asked to write in the 1983 issue of *Film Culture*, which contained a special Warren Sonbert tribute section. After praising his movies, I questioned his repetition of certain motifs, such as parades, circuses, elevated trains, car trips, be-ins, airplane wings, divas taking bows, which made each film begin to look like the outtakes of the previous one. (We might consider here the ethics of criticizing a friend in print. I told myself at the time that Warren was so surrounded by admirers, and that avant-garde film in general is so resistant to self-criticism that it was up to me to prod him toward taking up new challenges. I now see more clearly that this response was tied to a certain unconscious hostility and rivalry; I should have kept my doubts to myself. It is always a gamble to critique a friend's art, in public or private, and more often than not a mistake, but one I keep making, and will probably continue to make, driven as it is by vanity and laziness: the vanity is my misguided assumption that it is my job to be honest, and the laziness, that to tell the truth as I see it is easier for me than to modulate into another, more diplomatic if disingenuous way of responding.)

Warren replied to my criticism in the same issue. He bristled at the term *diary-film*, which he thought too suggestive of accidental, unintentional composition, but noted that he relied on the materials of his daily life: 'There are certain things that interest me, and that's what I film. People think that when they see new work of mine that I'm using out-takes from past films, things from seven, eight years ago. But I'll always go to the circus during a given period of film-making, or a parade, things that are out there on public display. But at the same time, the opposite of that – private, intimate things with friends, what they'll do at home, leisure, etc.'

It was a good answer: How much does anyone's daily life change from year to year? But it didn't answer my underlying reservation, which could have applied to many other experimental filmmakers besides Warren: that the need to assert a recognizable, avant-garde-approved identity led to the too-narrow refinement of a style, and that the general public's indifference toward experimental filmmaking promoted a too-cozy, uncritical appreciation within the beleaguered ranks.

As it happened, Warren did harbor dreams of making other, more ambitious films. He wrote a screenplay which he showed me for a feature film set in Nazi Germany, built around the premiere of Richard Strauss's opera *Capriccio*; but it was so intricate, with a dozen characters and as many locations, that it would have cost millions. Unable to raise the funding for it, he continued working on his self-contained, jewel-cut cantos, which I see in retrospect generously offered more than enough insight and beauty for any reasonable lover of film art. The cineaste in me is perfectly content with

Sonbert's oeuvre, especially knowing there will never be any more. At the time I wrote those comments in *Film Culture*, though, I was greedy. What we want from our gifted artist friends is – everything.

A stabilizing force had come into Warren's love life in the form of an older man, Ray. Immensely kind, cultivated, and knowledgeable about art, silver-mustached and rail-thin, securely employed, Ray became the protector, nurturer, devoted partner, and advocate whom Warren had long sought. They moved into another Victorian near Castro Street, which soon became a gathering place for their circle. Ray and Warren liked to entertain and give lavish dinner parties, and I had the privilege of attending a few when I was in the Bay Area. Living with Ray, Warren became more domestic. They traveled together, Ray shepherding Warren to his screenings in foreign cities, Warren indulging Ray's scholarly passion for tracking down Renaissance paintings. They had over ten happy years: in the best of circumstances, they would have grown old together. But Ray came down with AIDS and died.

Warren was bereft. Ray had been his lover, older brother, manager, and guardian angel. 'Who's going to take care of me now?' he said, with honest if brazen self-centeredness. In the year after Ray's death, Warren's friends, including myself, began to notice that he was becoming rather irritable and imperious, his temper flaring more readily. One would hear reports of his storming into projection booths and complaining about some technical flaw in the projection. He was acting more like a prima donna, which I see now must have been a side effect of his condition.

Warren began telling his friends that he was suffering from a mysterious disease. He insisted it was not AIDS but some baffling brain problem which eluded the physicians' diagnoses. He described to me episodes of passing out and being taken to the hospital, going through grueling tests, and finally being released. Knowing how Ray had died, I suspected early on that Warren was HIV-positive, but perhaps his pride could not bear admitting that he had been afflicted with the common scourge, rather than some rare, exotic ailment. A mutual friend who was very close to Warren noticed certain medications on his bureau and asked her physician-father about them. He confirmed that they were treatments for AIDS. She confronted Warren with this information, and he, still denying the fact, added testily: 'Well, given the fact that I'm gay and the life I've led, it wouldn't be surprising if I were suffering from AIDS!' It was classic Warren, wanting it both ways: to tell and not to tell. Perhaps he wanted to resist seeming pitiable in front of his friends. I had another friend who had acted similarly – gone off by himself to die back home in the Midwest, where his sister could nurse him, without telling his New York friends (especially his straight male friends, like me) he had AIDS. Regardless, I kept wishing Warren would trust me enough to tell me; but he stonewalled everyone, until close to the end.

The last few times I saw Warren, he made an effort to keep it light. He had hooked up with a young Hispanic named Ascension, who was looking after him and whom Warren, in turn, was educating in the finer points of life. They were running from one social engagement to another, seeing everyone and catching up with New York's cultural offerings. One day in early October, I got together with Warren for what turned out to be the last time. His speech sounded slurred from the drugs he was taking, and it was hard for him to stay on a subject; his attention kept wandering. He was most looking forward to the opera that night. He was wearing gray lederhosen with the hems rolled up, and he bragged about how he still kept going to the gym and his body looked great, all things considered – 'See, I'm unafraid to walk around in shorts in October, when most New Yorkers have already started bundling up.' I recalled his long-ago statement explaining the editing together of a Gay Pride parade and a graveyard shot: 'You know, "All is vanity." Those beautiful bodies will eventually be dust.' All is vanity, indeed, I thought: a step away from death, and he still has to show off his muscle tone? I have no doubt a gay man would have more sensitively approved the bravado behind Warren's wearing shorts, and seen it more intuitively as a species of courage.

Warren had to leave to introduce a screening of his

films at the Museum of Modern Art. After that, he and Ascension would go to the opera. 'Ciao,' he said amicably, walking up Fifty-Third Street to meet up with one of MOMA's curators, who would be waiting for him in the museum lobby.

Ciao. It will always seem too short, Warren's last good-bye, like an essay which ends with clumsy abruptness and you turn the page, thinking there must be another page that's missing. He who taught me the value of a gently graduated leave-taking was forced to make his own overly hasty exit from this life. We can stare at photographs of him, marveling at his jaunty presence, vitally bronzed as a movie star, yet detached, contrapposto, head turned away from the torso, away from us, and try to grapple with the paradox that someone can still be so alive to us and yet – gone. It is like one of those cruel facts he alluded to with his titles, *Rude Awakening*, *Divided Loyalties*, *Friendly Witness*, *Honor and Obey*, something he was trying to tell us all along.

# – 'Howl' and Me –

I have to say that 'Howl' struck me from the first as a little ludicrous and overblown. I must have been fourteen and still in junior high school, around 1957, when I first encountered Allen Ginsberg's groundbreaking poem. How it crossed my path I'm not sure; probably my brother, Leonard, who was seventeen and mad about García Lorca and Blake, tossed it my way, as he did all of his poetic discoveries. We went around for weeks intoning favorite passages – the first two lines, of course, 'I saw the best minds of my generation . . .' down to 'looking for an angry fix', and 'fucked in the ass by saintly motorcyclists, and screamed with joy' and 'boxcars boxcars boxcars', which for some reason always cracked us up. We loved the poem for its phonic fireworks and flaming images, but we also mocked its solemn oracular quality, applying an adolescent penchant for parody to any target within easy reach.

Much as we embraced Kerouac and Ginsberg as a retort to the 'tranquilized fifties', we were not immune to the ubiquitous parodies of the Beats in popular culture. Who could not giggle at Bob Hope's beatnik routine, wearing a beret and a fake goatee, banging bongos, snapping his fingers, and crying 'Yeah, man!'

Still, we were much more pro- than anti-Beat; and 'Howl', by virtue of giving America the finger, fit neatly into our bag of anarchic provocations, along with *Mad* magazine, the raunchier lyrics of rhythm and blues, Mort Sahl and Lenny Bruce.

Some shards of Ginsberg's dangerous shrapnel lodged more deeply in my subconscious than I realized, because, soon after reading it, I wrote a poem called 'I Hate It All' and turned it in to my English teacher for creative writing extra credit. This lurid rant enlisted every cliché about 'gnawing rats', 'crying men', and 'the dirt of the slums', disguising my personal resentment, no doubt, at my parents for making us live in a ghetto, before coming to the noble realization, 'But I am of it, of this thing I hate.' It was, if you will, a precociously James Baldwinish moment of identification with all I was trying to flee. My English teacher, Miss Loftus, responded with sour surprise, 'Phillip, I thought you were one of our most well-adjusted students!' and sent me down to the guidance counselor.

You must understand that, for all my extracurricular dabbling in anarchic culture, I was pretty much a *good* boy, and had gotten myself elected student president, no mean feat in a mostly black school, so that, when I began poetically denouncing the squalor of my immediate environment, the adults grew alarmed. Getting sent to the guidance counselor was not the pat-on-the-head, extra-credit response I had anticipated. I found myself in a jam, needing to explain my ode to hate as somehow not really reflective of my true feelings, and I began saying it was a creative put-on, spouting show-off references to the Dadaists and Surrealists. My dodge, I could tell, did not convince the guidance counselor; but she had no choice, given my refusal to admit what was really bothering me, except to send me back to class.

The odd thing, I see now, is that I kept doing this, modeling the role of the perfectly calm, responsible, civic-minded A student, while sending out flares that something was not right inside. In high school, I again got myself elected to office, this time chief justice of the student court, meanwhile writing a provoking piece about my feelings of alienation for a citywide essay contest. When my high school English teacher, Mrs Gold, accused me of trying to shock the middle class (she used, for the first time in my hearing, the French expression *épater le bourgeoisie*), I mocked her behind her back as a provincial spoilsport. I wanted to express honestly a little part of my adolescent confusion, darkness, and dread, while protecting my privacy by pretending I was merely being literary and experimental.

All this self-divided behavior culminated in my getting accepted to Columbia on a full scholarship, and trying to kill myself sophomore year. The combination of virginal frustration, too much Dostoevsky and Nietzsche, poverty, poor diet, finding myself adrift living away from home for the first time in the maddeningly impersonal and competitive atmosphere of

Columbia of those years combusted with my own neurotic impatience to yield the conclusion that life was not worth living. The point is that I knew more than I cared to admit about the screaming rage and shock expressed by 'Howl'; I had my own personal howl going on inside my head, and I was trying to keep a tight lid on it.

Having survived this adolescent crisis of yearning and negation, I would spend the rest of my life striving for skepticism and stoicism. You might say I turned away from 'Howl', with its suicidal grandiosity, gutter ecstasies, and apocalyptic nightmares, trading them in for the smaller promise of humor, equilibrium, and the everyday (i.e., don't take yourself so seriously). Allen Ginsberg, fellow Jewish writer and a Columbia dropout, was like an older brother (exactly seventeen years older) who had pioneered a path not to be taken. I would stay in college and guard my scholarship, graduate in four years, and get married at twenty, eager to show everyone what a mature, responsible fellow I was for my age.

The strongest pull that 'Howl' exerted on me thus was cautionary. If it seemed an advertisement for madness, drug addiction, vagrancy, homosexuality, and rhetoric as the road to enlightenment, I knew that those were not for me. Ginsberg might romanticize madness, saying: 'I'm with you in Rockland / where you scream in a straightjacket' or 'bang on the catatonic piano the soul is innocent' while awaiting 'fifty more shocks.' I had come close – too close – to ending up like Carl Solomon in Rockland State Hospital: having landed in the St. Luke's psych ward after my suicide attempt, I'd suddenly needed to convince the staff that I was perfectly all right, I did not require any shock treatment, thank you. Needles had always terrified me, so becoming a junkie held no appeal. I was dead set on clawing my way out of ghetto Brooklyn and into the middle class, too close to the poverty line to entertain romantic notions about bums and clochards. Limited as my sexual repertoire was, I did not want to get fucked in the ass by anyone, much less 'saintly motorcyclists'. And why 'saintly'? I'd seen Marlon Brando in *The Wild One* and the motorcycle gangs in *Scorpio Rising*, and real live Hells Angels menacing the Lower East Side, and not a scintilla of sanctity did they radiate. If Allen Ginsberg wanted to have an orgasm with a guy, fine with me, but why insist that it was saintly, or that the sailors who blew him were 'human seraphim'; that part struck me as sentimental. Besides, why was a good Jewish boy like Allen bothering with all that Christian-saint imagery? Perhaps the 'saintly' bothered me more than the 'motorcyclists'. (I'm not sure I thought that then, but I do now.)

'Howl' proffered one more temptation which I resisted mightily, and which was contained in the words 'my generation'. This may not be the proper occasion to explore what lies behind my distrust of that (to my mind) smug, self-mythologizing notion. Oh, what the hell. To quote Ben Hecht: 'It is, as I have long suspected, very difficult for a writer to write about anybody but himself.' Certainly true for me. In any case, I find the words 'my generation' presumptuous; I don't feel it's my right to generalize for all those who happened to be born during the same decade as myself. Or perhaps it isn't humility but vanity that won't allow me to speak of myself in any but idiosyncratic terms, resisting sociological categories that would place me in a collective epoch. Or am I merely envious that I never belonged to a glittering artistic set, like the Parisians around Picasso in Roger Shattuck's *Banquet Years*, or the Harvard crowd who went on to constitute the New York School of Poetry? Here was Ginsberg, lovingly canonizing his particular set of friends ('Holy Peter holy Allen holy Solomon holy Lucien holy Kerouac holy Huncke holy Burroughs holy Cassady') as not only a generation but 'the best minds of' his generation. And what entitled them to this accolade? That they ran naked through 'the negro streets', smoked dope on rooftops, dropped out of the academy – in other words, that they made a mess of their lives. Am I being too literal here? Are we supposed to think that they started off as the best minds of their generation, and then the evil capitalist Moloch society ruined them, or was it their own exquisite sensitivity that brought them to collapse?

Throughout the poem, Ginsberg seems torn between portraying his buddies as the divinely chosen accursed ones, maudits, and extending a more democratic laurel of beatitude to all the downtrodden and losers, as when he says 'holy Cassady holy the unknown buggered and suffering beggars holy the hideous human angels!' What about all those working stiffs who would not end up raving lunatics, who could not afford to drop out – were we automatically judged mediocre, and condemned to a lower status than 'the best minds', by dint of neglecting or refusing to fall apart? Of course 'Howl' is a young man's poem, and maybe I ought not to be subjecting it to this querulous, middle-aged class analysis when what it has most to recommend it is its jazzy, generative enthusiasm, and its wholesome desire for redemptive embrace. The poem ends with these lines:

> Holy forgiveness! mercy! charity! faith! Holy! Ours!
>     bodies! suffering! magnanimity!
> Holy the supernatural extra brilliant intelligent kindness
>     of the soul!

Okay, I can buy that. Not sure what it means, but I'm all for kindness and forgiveness. Where I have trouble is when the poet says: 'the soul is innocent'. He invokes the word *innocence* several times in 'Howl', like a son pleading before a stern father-judge, demanding amnesty for all self-destructive acts, and shifting the blame disingenuously onto Society, Moloch. Why not accept that we are not innocent?

Well, that is one reading of the poem, and probably the most conventional one. A contrary reading would be that Ginsberg himself was something of a detached observer, more stable than the others, portraying clearly though with sympathy the screwups of those around him, even envying them their loss of control, yet in his own way being cautionary, undeceived by their pitiable attempts to rationalize all that insane behavior – and cautious himself, getting on with the business of a literary career. For instance, is there not some irony when he speaks of those 'who threw potato salad at CCNY lecturers on Dadaism and subsequently presented themselves on the granite steps of the madhouse with shaven heads and harlequin speech of suicide, demanding instantaneous lobotomy'? Or when he refers to 'Dreams! adorations! illuminations! religions! the whole boatload of sensitive bullshit!' Yes, the whole boatload of sensitive bullshit. That is what 'Howl' throws at us, and also what the poem attempts to surmount – and it manages, at times, to have it both ways.

I will always be grateful to 'Howl' for preparing me for the beauties of Walt Whitman, whose cornucopic inventories and one-line portraits seem both gorgeous and inevitable. These two American masters share a love of cities and public spaces, the undersides of bridges, the streets, rooftops, alleys – the whole consoling urbanistic shebang – as when Ginsberg conjures up those who faded out in vast sordid movies, were shifted in dreams, woke on a sudden Manhattan, and picked themselves up out of basements hung-over with heartless Tokay and horrors of Third Avenue iron dreams & stumbled to unemployment offices.

These days when I read 'Howl', I forgive the Blakean seraphic bluster and attend to the superb atmospherics of place, which mean more to me the older I grow.

The poem of Ginsberg's that really floored me was 'Kaddish'. I could be indifferent, finally, to 'Howl''s Carl Solomon rotting in Rockland's mental wards, indifferent to Neal Cassady's priapic triumphs ('secret hero of these poems, cocksman and Adonis of Denver –'), but I could not be indifferent to Naomi, given my own embarrassed love for a difficult mother.

Years later, when I was a fellow traveler of the New York School of Poetry, I would run into Ginsberg at parties and readings. We gave each other a wide berth; he seemed much more interested in cute young boys than in my own person, and I, for my part, did not go out of my way to cultivate him, the more so as I drifted away from a bohemian mind-set. Instead I added him to that list of famous writers I knew casually but was unable to bring myself to cultivate, which I now only partly regret.

Once, after the Stonewall riots in 1969, I volunteered my services to a benefit poetry reading for gay rights, thinking it important for straight writers such as myself to show solidarity publicly with the gay community. I read a long, comic, mother-son poem that night called 'The Blue Pants', and Ginsberg closed the reading with some new poems. Afterward, he came up and told me I should have read a little faster. What a *putz*! I thought. Here I was 'magnanimously' going out of my heterosexual way to participate in a gay rights reading, and he was criticizing my delivery. Years later, I wonder if he may have been paying me a compliment: recognizing a fellow entertainer, though one much less experienced than he, and giving me a bit of professional advice. I probably *should* have read the poem a touch faster.

In 1984, I was on a committee to select the Pulitzer Prize in poetry. The Pulitzer is decided in two stages: first the writers' committee goes through all the nominated books in its designated area and sends up three recommendations, then a group of newspaper and magazine editors makes the final selection. Since the editors are usually not as well-versed in poetry as one might wish, they often pick the most conventional, user-friendly collection. In any event, I pushed hard for Allen Ginsberg's *Collected Poems: 1947–1980* to be named one of the three finalists. It was a huge volume, eight-hundred-plus pages, and of course inconsistent in quality, but the high points were amazing: that Ginsberg was a major American poet of towering achievement seemed self-evident. I did not, however, succeed in convincing the other two literary judges to include him (there was still that curious fussiness about Ginsberg's coloring outside the lines of the well-made poem), so I took the unusual step of filing a minority recommendation, obliging the editors who would have final decision to consider his *Collected*, along with books by the other three finalists (Carolyn Kizer, Charles Wright, and Robert Duncan). As it turned out, the editors also rejected Ginsberg for the Pulitzer, choosing Kizer. By this time Ginsberg and I had developed a friendly nodding acquaintance, and had spoken a few times on the phone. I phoned Allen at his home to tell him he had at least been one of the finalists. He was philosophical about it, saying, 'They don't want to give the big prizes to me. They still hold against me all that stuff from the sixties.'

I suppose you can be either King of the May or Poet Laureate, but not both in the same lifetime. By now he was elderly and infirm, and we chatted for fifteen minutes, mostly about his ailments, but also about teaching creative writing. (He knew I had been active in the writer-in-the-schools movement.) I don't remember anything specifically that he said – nothing except for the tone, which was extremely amiable. He struck me as a nice guy, a sweet, elderly, realistic Jew of a sort I was familiar with from my youth, and I chastised myself for having misjudged him before as a *putz*.

The truth is that he was probably both, a *mensch* and a *putz*.

I may have misjudged 'Howl', and am probably

misjudging it still. How to evaluate such a torrent with objectivity? That poem is lodged in my psyche, at the crossroads of my adolescent confusions, and I can't be too hard on myself for failing to see it clearly or extract it from that tumult.

# – The Poetry Years –

For about fifteen years I wrote poetry. I published poems in countless little magazines, gave readings all over, earned a living of sorts as a poet in the schools, teaching the art to children, and put out two collections: the first in 1972, the second in 1976. When I look back at those years during which being a poet formed such an important part of my identity, I am tempted to rub my eyes, as though recalling a time when I ran off and joined the circus.

How had I started writing poetry in the first place? I can honestly say I had no early ambitions along those lines. True, in elementary school I was by default the class poet, just as there was a boy who drew horses well and another boy who ran fleetly at Field Day. When Thanksgiving approached, I would be expected to craft a few stanzas about the Pilgrims' feast. In junior high I wrote several tortured poems under the Beats' influence. But by high school I had forsaken poetry for prose: I was going to be a novelist.

In college, joining the literary circle around *Columbia Review*, I befriended the poet Ron Padgett. The Oklahoma-born Padgett and I had heard of each other by freshman rumor, circling each other like two gunfighters; he had even put the word out through mutual friends that he was going to break my butt. I, having hailed from the streets of Brooklyn, let it be known he was welcome to try. Of course when we finally met, no fisticuffs occurred: he showed me a superb paper he had written for English about Pound and the medieval troubadours, I showed him a paper on Yeats, and we were off to the races.

Padgett had precociously started a poetry magazine back in high school, writing to poets he admired for contributions; and he came to New York to attend Columbia in 1960 as part of a Tulsa émigré gang that also included Ted Berrigan, Joe Brainard, and Dick Gallup, and that affixed themselves to the New York School of Poetry. The charismatic Kenneth Koch, who taught in the English Department, had lured Padgett and friends to Columbia. I attended the lunchtime readings Koch gave of his own poetry, and a memorable one of Bad Poetry, which he delivered with chortling oratory. Koch embodied what struck me as a refreshing, zany poetics that drew equally on comic strips, mock-epic parodies of Ariosto, and Dada game structures. I would later come to revere him as one of the most farsighted poets of our era, and in the last decade of his life we became friends; but as an undergraduate I was too intimidated to take a course from him. So I settled for becoming a prose-writing hanger-on of the New York School of Poetry, with entrée to the scene provided by Ron Padgett, all of us worshiping at the shrine of Koch, Frank O'Hara, and John Ashbery.

The one whose poetry appealed to me most at that time was Frank O'Hara, partly because of his unapologetically urban, movie-mad sensibility, partly because of his doctrine of Personalism:

> You just go on nerve. If someone's chasing you down the street with a knife you just run, you don't turn around and shout, 'Give it up! I was a track star for Mineola Prep.' . . . How can you really care if anybody gets it, or gets what it means, or if it improves them? Improves them for what? For death? Why hurry them along? Too many poets act like a middle-aged mother trying to get her kids to eat too much cooked meat, and potatoes with drippings (tears). I don't give a damn whether they eat or not. Forced feeding leads to excessive thinness (effete). Nobody should experience anything they don't need to, if they don't need poetry bully for them. I like the movies too. And after all, only Whitman and Crane and Williams, of the American poets, are better than the movies. As for measure and other technical apparatus, that's just common sense: if you're going to buy a pair of pants you want them to be tight enough so everyone will want to go to bed with you.

His example gave casual permission to construct a poem out of anything at hand, from a friend's remark to a movie star's collapse to a headline or honking car or sudden mood change.

Just as there was a *politique des auteurs* among

film buffs, so a sort of *politique des poètes* existed, with battle lines drawn between the more Establishment, prize-winning poets of the day, such as Robert Lowell, Richard Wilbur, John Berryman, Elizabeth Bishop, Richard Eberhart, Anthony Hecht, and Anne Sexton, and the New York School, who drew their inspiration from the French modernist poets and the painting of Willem de Kooning, Larry Rivers, and Jane Freilicher. Koch's poem 'Fresh Air' was a manifesto that thumbed its nose at everything solemn, high-minded, ethically worrying – 'academic', in a word – and called for a poetics of sensuous, playful experimentation. In it, he ridiculed poetry 'Written by the men with their eyes on the myth / And the Missus and the midterms, in the *Hudson Review*.'

Of course these divisions grew fuzzier the closer you examined the matter: Koch himself taught at Columbia, and who could be wittier or more linguistically playful than Richard Wilbur? But there still seemed this antagonism as between opposing teams, the one (the so-called Established writers) using poetry as a tragic criticism of life, the other (the New York School) as a giddy celebration of art. I remember visiting Ted Berrigan in his East Village pad, and being told by him that he never mixed life with art. Art came from art, he said, not life. Anyone reading Ted's heartbreaking, autobiographical Sonnets (or O'Hara's personal poems, for that matter) would be hard-pressed to concur with his assertion, but that was at least the party line.

When I first read the poetry of Berryman, Lowell, Bishop, Sexton, and Sylvia Plath, I felt guilty, like a Catholic reading books on the Index, and even guiltier for liking them so much. Lowell's *Life Studies* was a revelation to me, with its acerbic honesty ('Tamed by *Miltown*, we lie on Mother's bed'); Berryman's *Dream Songs* a grim delight ('Life, friends, is boring. We must not say so.'). Surely it was possible to like both anguished confessional and breezy diaristic poetry? But I kept my taste for the former under wraps around the New York School crowd.

I remember attending a reading by Ashbery at NYU around 1967, when he premiered some of the brilliant poems from *Rivers and Mountains*. Perhaps to distance himself from the prophetic, baton style of Robert Duncan or the shamanistic intoning of Allen Ginsberg, Ashbery read his poems with an ironic disdain, as if he had just bent down and picked up a piece of trash that had some improbable gibberish written on it:

*These decibels*
*Are a kind of flagellation, an entity of sound*
*Into which being enters, and is apart.*
*Their colors on a warm February day*
*Make for masses of inertia, and hips*
*Prod out of the violet-seeming into a new kind*
*Of demand that stumps the absolute because not new*
*In the sense of the next one in an absolute series*

*But, as it were, pre-existing or pre-seeming in*
*Such a way as to contrast funnily with the unexpectedness*
*And somehow push us all into perdition.*

I had no idea what any of it meant, but I liked listening to its tantalizing flashes of music and meaning. Afterward, I hung around long enough to get invited to the cocktail party. At parties after New York School poetry readings, you would receive your literary marching orders. Reading tips were offered within an acceptably avant-garde framework that included such writers as Gertrude Stein, William S. Burroughs, Ronald Firbank. When I spoke to Ashbery after the reading, he recommended to me de Chirico's *Hebdomeros* and Raymond Roussel's *Impressions of Africa*, both hieratic texts in a Surrealist vein, and the relatively obscure poets F. T. Prince and John Wheelwright. I later came to suspect he was throwing acolytes off the scent, and that he himself had perhaps been more deeply influenced by Wordsworth, Bishop, and Auden.

Myself, I could not get enough of *Rivers and Mountains*, and read it until the spine cracked. Later, in 1968, when I began writing poetry, I spent a fruitless summer trying to imitate Ashbery's elegant opacity. No one could have shown less aptitude for writing in the Ashbery mode than I, given my penchant for the straightforward; but he was the most influential poet of the period, and so I had at least to give it a try.

What I took from my days as a New York Poetry

School fellow traveler was less aesthetic than social. I had the privilege to watch the way a lively poetry scene mushroomed at St. Mark's Church in-the-Bowery, in the East Village, under the nurturance of the Poetry Project's director, the glamorous Anne Waldman (she had even acted in television's *The Mod Squad*). This was the closest I would ever come to being part of a literary circle, a generation, a movement, a bohemia, and though I have always considered myself a loner, it gave me a clear glimpse of how such a network functioned. I accepted the poets' generous invitations to parties, to passed joints, to publications in mimeo magazines, to friendships and acquaintanceships. What they made of me I have no idea. My first wife, Carol, and I lived way uptown, at the northern end of Manhattan above the Cloisters: one time we threw a party and invited the St. Mark's crowd to it, though they seemed wary ever of venturing above Fourteenth Street. They arrived late, having brought with them on the A train enough reading matter for an ocean crossing. Immediately they headed for the bedroom to get stoned, ignoring my other friends. But if the St. Mark's poets were insular, they were also warmly loyal. I was fascinated by the way they supported each other. I once asked Ron Padgett how he and Ted Berrigan critiqued one another's poems. 'I just say, "That's totally terrific, Ted," and when I show him mine he says, "That's totally terrific, Ron" to me,' he answered. Whether this was strictly true I have my doubts, but the lesson seemed to be that critical fussiness was passé. Another time I was visiting the poet/ future art critic Peter Schjeldahl in his apartment, and I commented with surprise that he kept WABC, a Top 40 rock station, on all the time. What did he do when bad songs played on the air? Schjeldahl said obstinately, 'There are no bad rock songs today.' Was he pulling my leg, or did he really believe that? I felt like a visitor from the nineteenth century.

I also watched with surprise and maybe some envy how the poets and their mates swapped partners. Ted Berrigan read a poem at St. Mark's Church that went something like: 'When you sleep with your best friend's wife / She gets fucked / He gets fucked / And you get fucked.' Loud titters were heard from the cognoscenti, who knew the poem's other referents, both of whom were in the audience that night.

As eye-opening as all this was, it did not necessarily make me want to be a poet. That came about another way.

Living on the brink of poverty, I was looking for some freelance editorial work (often a euphemism for ghostwriting, which I did extensively during this period), when I came upon a notice requesting readers to help edit a new poetry anthology. Reading was one thing I felt sure I could do; I did very little else. So I answered the ad and was summoned to an interview at the home of one Hyman Sobiloff.

Mr Sobiloff, often referred to in those days as 'the businessman-poet', was a wealthy venture capitalist who lived in a very tony town house on East Seventy-Seventh Street in the Upper East Side. He had several servants, and his town house had its own elevator, which impressed the hell out of me. A Chinese servant answered the door, brought me into the parlor, and told me to wait, as Mr Sobiloff was just getting up. (This was noon.) I had time to examine the antiques and indifferent paintings before the great man himself appeared, in a silk striped robe: his fleshy, curt, bald-headed, imperial manner put me instantly in mind of Louis Calhern in *The Asphalt Jungle*, some sort of mobster kingpin or political boss (Calhern also played the title role in *Julius Caesar*). Sobiloff explained the nature of the project, which was to revise the immensely popular poetry anthologies that had been edited by his late friend Oscar Williams. I was happy to tell him my own mother had read aloud from them to us, when we were children, such favorites as Alfred Noyes's 'The Highwayman'. Poetically, you might say, Oscar Williams's anthologies were mother's milk to me. Sobiloff gruffly cut me off, saying the point was that they needed to be updated. He had undertaken the chore as an act of devotion to a friend who'd passed away. He pointed to several precipitously tall stacks of poetry books on French Empire chairs and said, 'I know all this stuff cold, but I can't be bothered to go through 'em, I'm too busy. I need an assistant.' Somehow I doubted he was as familiar with the contents of these volumes as he pretended, but I played along, familiar as I was with my ghostwriting clients' need to pretend omniscience. On my end, I bluffed like crazy about my knowledge of poetry. The interview lasted fifteen minutes. He seemed satisfied; we agreed on a salary, and I took away a few shopping bags full of books.

I had now to educate myself as quickly as possible in the English and American poetic canon. I was overwhelmed by the vast amounts of poetry I would have to absorb, but I began by plowing through the original Oscar Williams anthologies. I quickly saw that Oscar had put his friend Hy in the books, as he had his own wife, Gene Derwood, and himself, though their verse hardly seemed in the same league as that of Keats and Whitman. Sobiloff, I learned, was philanthropically active, and a heavy supporter of poetry societies and magazines. I was too shy to ask Sobiloff how he had made his millions, but someone in the know told me that he had started in the furniture business, and had perfected a scheme of buying a second, failing business and transferring all the assets from the first failing business to the second, then shutting that down and transferring all the assets of the second to a third . . . in any case, some kind of fiscal legerdemain.

Shortly after beginning the job, I learned I was not the only poetry reader; Sobiloff had hired two others, like a gambler placing bets across the board. At first he kept us strictly separate; but in time I was able to contact them, and consolidate my position as First Reader, *primus inter pares*, by offering to coordinate the project for a higher fee. He appreciated my ruthlessness, I think. It was Sobiloff who said once in passing that he was flying off to vacation in Barbados, leaving the city because 'I'm tired of all those ghetto faces', a statement so appalling to me that I was almost charmed by its brazenness. I myself came from the ghetto and wondered when he would ferret out that fact. On another visit to the boss, I met a lady friend of his whom I took to be his mistress, a woman in her fifties with the body of an ex-showgirl and a face that looked like it had seen everything. When Sobiloff left the room for a minute she warned me not to take advantage of her Hy, if I knew what was good for me.

Believe me, I had no intention of cutting corners. My work schedule consisted of reading four poetry books a day minimum. Most of them came from the library, some from used book stores – our boss had given us permission to augment his limited stock, and I saved the receipts for him. I would wake up and eat breakfast while starting on the first, get dressed, finish reading the book, take some notes about possible selections, and go off for a walk with a bag lunch around noontime, often ending on a bench in Riverside Park (my wife and I had by this time moved down from Inwood to West 104th Street, near Columbia), where I would read a second book, and then begin paging through a third . . . By now I was starting to feel headachy from eye strain and nauseous from a surfeit of poetic expressiveness, so I would give it a rest, then turn to book four in the late afternoon, and maybe book five that evening, if I had anything left in me. I recommend this brutal pedagogic method of saturation reading to anyone with literary ambition. Overstuffed like a goose for the manufacture of foie gras, I had no choice but to secrete my own poems. Out of sheer survival I needed to have my say.

Two other factors, besides the anthology reader gig, sparked my entry into poetry in the years I am describing, 1967–69: the political upheaval of the antiwar movement and the breakdown of my marriage. They were not unrelated. Living as we did fairly close to Columbia University, I got swept up in the 1968 student revolt and reentered my old alma mater as a troublemaking alumnus. Just as I had been a hanger-on at the New York School of Poetry scene, so now I became a fellow traveler of the New Left, participating in demonstrations, political meetings, and study groups, reading Marxist texts alongside all that poetry. I never felt entirely comfortable with my posture of radicalism, nor could I embrace deep down the hope of making revolution, being an ex-scholarship kid from the ghetto still trying to crawl into the middle class. But the heady sixties talk of sexual liberation and down-with-the-bourgeoisie and smashing monogamy had a destabilizing effect on my domestic arrangements. Not that I can blame the failure of that first marriage on the revolutionary Left. I had married too young, at twenty, and hadn't a clue; we both made our mistakes.

Meanwhile, my first novel had not found a publisher; it was intensely embarrassing to have a sympathetic witness to my failure living in the same apartment with me. I was unable to take defeat in stride and start on a second one. Writing novels requires a calm, settled, bourgeois existence, and the payoff is deferred for years. The fragmentation I felt so painfully in those days would not permit me to submerge myself again in a prolonged alternate dream-narrative: I was too antsy, too much at the mercy of jittery day-to-day reality. I needed a form I could turn to with quicker results, snatching a few hours here and there from a patched-together freelance existence and the emotional confusion of whether to leave or stay. Hence, poetry.

My first poems seemed to emerge from conjugal dilemma. I still hoped we could salvage the marriage, if we both behaved responsibly and maturely. (Yeah, right.) These poems now strike me as tentative and hypocritical, the way a couple in their last stage bullshit during marriage counseling while secretly eyeing the exit. Formally, I was feeling my way into poetry at the same time I was feeling my way out of the marriage. By the time our marriage had definitively collapsed, I was on much firmer ground. Incidentally, I have always derived poetic inspiration from breakups. The rejection of love produces an emotional clarity in me, while the return to solitude arouses a need to solace myself, with either lyrical resignation or revenge.

I had decided to leave Carol and New York for California, the promised land of youth culture. Before I decamped, I turned in my lists of recommendations for the updated anthologies. It's funny to recall what I thought then would make for such substantial improvements. I had wanted the collections to seem less stuffy, so I added Bessie Smith and Bob Dylan lyrics, and Native American chants, and a slew of black poets, and of course increased the selections of the New York School poets, and F. T. Prince, John Wheelwright, Robert Creeley, George Oppen, Ed Dorn, and Allen Ginsberg, among others. Sobiloff looked them over without saying a word. Years later, when the revised anthologies appeared, I had a hard time finding any evidence of my labors. But the job had served its purpose: it had given me a condensed poetic education.

The poets who influenced me the most at the beginning of my poetic career were William Carlos Williams, Frank O'Hara, Pablo Neruda, Vladimir Mayakovsky, and Randall Jarrell. I was happy to purloin Williams's three-line stanzas, or O'Hara's splattering of words across the page; to imitate Mayakovsky's mock-megalomaniac outbursts, Neruda's surreal inventories, or the loquacity of late Jarrell. Later on I would fall in love with the dramatic monologues at the back of Pasternak's novel *Doctor Zhivago*, and Cavafy's deceptively simple lyrics and history poems, and Pavese's *Hard Labor*, with its dense materialist details of working-class life.

I was searching for something that made me happy whenever I found it, but I still didn't know how to characterize it. Though I had been a fan of Neruda's, when I attended a reading of his at the Ninety-Second Street Y, he put me off with his hammy, amphitheater delivery. It was another Chilean poet, Nicanor Parra, who crystallized for me what I was looking for, with the title of his collection *Poems and Antipoems*. This taste for 'antipoetry', for grubby reality, was addressed by Wallace Stevens in his preface to the 1934 *Collected Poems* by William Carlos Williams, when he described Williams as someone for whom 'the anti-poetic is that truth, that reality to which all of us are forever fleeing'. I was drawn to the antipoetic for a number of reasons. First, my training had been in fiction, and I was still charmed by the sound of conversational prose. Though literary critics might disparage a poem as being 'chopped-up prose', that was insufficient to condemn it in my eyes. Quite the contrary: it interested me, perversely, to see how far one could go in that direction and still get away with it. A storyteller at heart, I also continued to like narrative. Some of Parra's and Cavafy's poems were like little short stories: a room, a memory, a pickup.

Second, I was much more intrigued by poetic statement than by metaphor, simile, and image. When

I heard it said that great poets were characterized by their gift for metaphor, it bugged me. I did not go out of my way to find metaphors; if an apt one swam into my brain while I was writing a poem, I put it in; if not, not. A profusion of metaphor and simile seemed to me, at this point in my poetry writing, forced. I even developed a theory that the late manner of certain poets, such as Pasternak and Montale, favored unadorned poetic statement, because they no longer felt the need to show off with metaphors in order to prove their poetic bona fides.

Third, I was rebelling against the lingering idea that poems should contain language or ideas that were suitably 'poetic' – the beauties of nature, flowers, finches, rapture, elevated sentiment; I was drawn to a more sardonic poetry that would traffic in mundane commercial objects, business terms, legalese. It pleased me beyond measure to be able to use a word like *bicameral* in a poem on Allende. A city rat, I had no command of the names of flora and fauna, and needed to stake my claim with vocabulary that would verge on the prosaic and antiromantic.

Finally, being poetically self-taught and, despite having read many books on prosody, finding that very little of it stuck to me, never able to master my quantities, meters, and values, never having gone to graduate school to study poetry, I still composed poems largely intuitively, on the basis of what rhythms or combinations 'sounded right' to my ear. This awkward situation made me feel at a disadvantage among trained poets. But it also drove me to embrace the antipoetic tradition that ran like a heretical streak through poetic history. Essentially I was trying to turn a limitation (my ignorance) into a strength (my preference for the antipoetic).

To some degree, I was taking permission from the era's looser standards. The 1960s allowed for a wide open, pluralistic (some would say amateurish) poetics. The ascendance of the oral, from the Beats' first-word-best-word through the black activist rappers such as Gil Scott-Heron and the Last Poets, the cultural enthronement of rock troubadours, the proliferation of open readings and mimeo magazines, the promotion of children's poetry and ethnopoetics, all contributed to the idea that anyone could write poetry, or had the right to call himself a poet; one didn't need a graduate credential. It may have been an invitation to charlatanism and self-delusion, but it also made for a no-holds-barred, anything-goes freedom; and I suppose I sneaked in under that umbrella.

A key determinant for me during these years was becoming friends with the poet Bill Zavatsky, a friendship I am happy to say has lasted over forty years. Zavatsky is a largehearted, open, funny man and a very fine poet, as well as a capable jazz pianist. When I first met him around 1968, he was writing ebullient verse that ran arpeggios in all directions. His verbal fireworks showed the influence of the French Surrealists, particularly André Breton, whom he later translated. At the same time, he was trying to master a leaner lyric with more sincerity and humanity, to put more honest emotions, situations, and characters into his poems. Robert Lowell once commented that he found it hard to 'people' his poems. I, with my fiction background and interest in psychological cul-de-sacs, found that part relatively easy; my poetic struggles occurred on another plane. In any case, Zavatsky was drawn to what I was doing, and he encouraged me to keep writing situational, reality-based poems.

Zavatsky had recently gotten an MFA in poetry writing at Columbia, where he'd studied with Stanley Kunitz and Harvey Shapiro, and he introduced me to a circle of young Kunitz-Shapiro-trained poets, which included Hugh Seidman, Mark Rudman, and Louise Glück, who hung out at the West End Bar and other venues in Morningside Heights. Soon I was participating in their open readings. Through them I became familiar with another poetic model, the Objectivists (Oppen, Zukofsky, and Rakosi), and their younger allies, Shapiro, Armand Schwerner, and David Ignatow. I was particularly taken with the hard-bitten, wry, tight urban lyrics of Shapiro and Ignatow. Some of my poems seem to have come directly out of an attempt to write like them.

But the poet in the Objectivist orbit who came to affect me most was Charles Reznikoff. He was still alive then, though elderly, and had been rediscovered, championed by younger poets, who were as moved by his example of humility and noncareerism as by his spare, tender poems. Reznikoff had for years published his own verse, gone his own solitary way. He had fashioned a poetics of daily observation and reflection, taking long walks and then drafting his urban encounters into concise accounts in verse. His poems eschewed all verbal razzle-dazzle, yet they shimmered with a sympathy and humanity which never sentimentalized, including as they did the recognition of human cruelty. In person – I met him a number of times – and on the page, he had a quality of resignation or acceptance (which was it? both, perhaps) that suggested spiritual wisdom. And no one was more exposed to the charge of being prosaic or 'antipoetic'. His long-lined autobiographical sequence, 'Early History of a Writer', reads stubbornly close to chopped-up prose – an engrossing personal essay with a ragged right-hand margin.

What made him, in the end, truly poetic was his economical use of language and his limpid vision of reality, which might be compared to Bashō and Li Po:

*In the street, nine stories below, the horn of an automobile*
*out of order*
*began sounding its loudest*
*steadily – without having to stop for breath.*
*We tried to keep on talking*
*in spite of that unceasing scream;*

*raised our voices somewhat, no longer calm and serene.*
*Our civilization was somewhat out of order, it seemed.*

*But, just as we began to knit our brows,*
*tighten our jaws, twist our lips,*
*the noise stopped;*
*and we dipped our heads,*
*like ducks on a stream, into the cool silence,*
*and talked again quietly, smiling at each other.*

Reznikoff provided a solution to my guilt about not being able to achieve the proper (MFA-approved) poetic surface: I had only to write down what I saw, heard, and thought, as honestly as possible, and the poetry would take care of itself. The problem was that I could never be as pure a being as Reznikoff, and some of my attempts to write like him misfired from disingenuous oversimplicity. I also had an incurable taste for the ironic, rationalizing, or mischievously analytical narrator, which led me in distinctly non-Reznikoffian directions. But Reznikoff was never far off, once I had admitted him into my pantheon as a benign conscience, a figure of enduring through failure.

Two other, non-literary influences on my poetry during that time deserve mention. The first was psychotherapy. I was seeing a Jungian psychologist named George Romney, a Cuban émigré who smoked cigarillos and had wavy black hair and an infectious laugh; it became my secret goal to provoke that laugh of his as often as possible in sessions. I would tell him about my experiences, and sometimes in the midst of my relating them they would cohere into a kind of improvised poem, which would make him chuckle and which I would then go home and try to write down. In this way my long poem 'The Blue Pants' came about. George also frequently asked me, as therapists are wont to do, what I was feeling in the moment, directing my attention to the emotion physiologically manifesting and gurgling in my body. Out of this practice of attempting to pin down emotional states came poems such as 'Numbness', 'Not Sadness Which Is Always There', and 'Clearing a Space'. The very ambition to write poems anchored in the present moment – to open myself to the here-and-now, as it were – derived from techniques I'd been learning in psychotherapy.

The second crucial nonliterary influence on my poetry was teaching inner-city youth. I worked as a Poet in the Schools for over a dozen years, first helping high school dropouts in East Harlem get their equivalency degree, then directing a program for Teachers & Writers Collaborative at P.S. 75 in the Upper West Side of Manhattan. Along with my first published prose book, *Being with Children*, a number of poems resulted directly from that work experience, which also brought me closer to my own memories of childhood and early adolescence.

Teaching kids grew partly out of a desire to be socially useful: to put my political ideals into practice.

At the same time I was looking for ways to incorporate my politics into my poetry. In one case, I had been leafing through a picture book of Cuban revolutionary art, and I came upon a propaganda poster with the title 'Solidarity with Mozambique', and wondered how on earth I could ever feel my way into bonding with a struggle that seemed so far away and so abstract. I began writing about daily occurrences in New York City, then tried to reach, by concentric circles leading farther and farther away from myself, the rebels in Mozambique. (Not that I ever convincingly made it.) My poem 'Allende' required no such elaborate device: I was simply shaken by the overthrow of the Chilean leftist's government and wanted to register my dismay without resorting to the usual consoling *venceremos* clichés.

Finally, I took scraps from everything around me and built a poetic nest with them: movie references, which were hard to resist, given my lifelong cinephilia; musical refrains (I kept playing Lotte Lenya's album, and her crack-voiced rendition of 'Lost in the Stars' seeped into my bones); the economic recession and New York City default scare of 1975; the exploding gentrification that followed in my Upper West Side neighborhood; phone conversations with exes; the parade of failed romances and breakup scenes, always good for a poem.

Around 1977 I started writing personal essays and also went back to longer fiction. I see in retrospect that

I was handling the same material, the same themes, in poetry and prose. The single person learning to be alone is a theme sounded in many of the poems of this period no less than in the prose that makes up my first essay collection, *Bachelorhood*.

Regardless of the genre I happened to be working in, I found myself resisting the transcendent. I was skeptical of all triumphalism, both positive (redemption) and negative (apocalypse). I threw in my lot with ordinary life, 'the daily round'. This mistrust of transcendence was another way in which I felt myself out of step with the ideological presuppositions of much contemporary poetry. But again, I was trying to turn weakness into strength: the inability to reach the stars, to achieve anything like spiritual sublimity, became a stubborn claim that the earth is all we have – a brief for groundedness.

—

To go back to 1972: I had been amassing sufficient poems for a first collection when a printer based in Northampton approached me and offered to put them out in a chapbook. The plan was for me to spend the month of August at his print shop, learning to operate a letter press and assisting in the production of the book, to be entitled *The Eyes Don't Always Want to Stay Open*. When I arrived in Northampton, however, I discovered that the printer and his wife were about to divorce, and he was temporarily closing the business while they sorted out the division of conjugal assets. I was welcome, he said, to stay in their house for the month of August, now that it had been vacated by both husband and wife, each of whom had moved in with a new lover. As I had no other plans for summer vacation, I decided to stick it out and explore the town and the surrounding Massachusetts countryside. I was at first miserably lonely, and felt foolish and hollow. But as it happened, an elderly, poetry-loving woman neighbor befriended me. She knew how to operate the letter press. So we set in type exactly one of my poems, the paranoid epistle 'We Who Are Your Closest Friends', as a broadside. (Anne Lamott, to my surprise, included this poem in her popular writing manual, *Bird by Bird*, thus bringing it to thousands of readers it would otherwise not have reached.)

Returning to the city, discouraged that there would be no chapbook after all, I visited Bill Zavatsky and his wife, Phyllis, the first night back, hoping they might cheer me up. Zavatsky, who edited the poetry magazines *SUN* and *Roy Rogers*, had been mulling over the idea of starting his own line of poetry books. Seeing me so disappointed, he told me not to worry; he would put out my collection himself. To my astonished gratitude he began retyping the manuscript immediately, and stayed up half the night finishing the job, while I slept (more or less) on his couch. Thus was born SUN Press, which would publish Padgett, Harvey Shapiro, Jaimy Gordon, Paul Violi, Raymond Roussel, Paul Auster, and Zavatsky himself, but whose maiden publication was *The Eyes Don't Always Want to Stay Open.* My second collection, *The Daily Round*, would follow in 1976.

What remains to be told is how or why I gave up writing poetry. There is a simple answer and a complicated one. First the simple one:

In 1980 I moved to Houston, Texas, to teach at the University of Houston. I had been recruited as the creative writing program's first prose writer, on the basis of my memoir about teaching, *Being with Children*, my novel *Confessions of Summer*, and my soon-to-be-released personal essay collection, *Bachelorhood.* If in New York City I had been accepted as a poet, such was not the case in Houston. I was not permitted to teach poetry courses. I need not have taken it personally: my colleagues Rosellen Brown and Ntozake Shange, both of whom had published two poetry books as well but were hired as prose writers, faced the same prohibition in that university writing program.

A higher, 'purer' standard of what it took to be a poet seemed to reign over that corner of academia, based partly on the possession of an MFA credential, and partly on the networking of the professional poetry world. I got a real taste of the way the poetry guild mentality operated: the mentoring and bestowal of the blessing on a chosen few acolytes, whose books would then be lobbied for publication. The nonexclusionary ethos of the sixties and early seventies had ended in the face of the writing program-generated mystique of technique. The impression was conveyed that the poet was someone like a prophet, of rare vatic powers, and there could only be at most two dozen poets in an era who'd received the vision. I knew I'd never gotten a message from on high: I did not fit that bill. My sense of myself as a poet began to shrivel up.

But that simple explanation is false. It would be wrong to blame my colleagues for killing the urge, since anyone who can be discouraged so easily from writing poetry is not cut out to be a poet. The truth is that I had already begun moving away from poetry before I came down to Houston, having fallen in love with the personal essay and its possibilities. I found in the personal essay a wonderful plasticity, which combined the storytelling aspects of fiction with the lyrical, associative qualities of poetry. If, as Robert Bly recommended, American poets should learn to 'leap' freely from line to line, thought to thought, and subject to subject, I realized I could do that as easily in the personal essay as in a poem. Moreover, I could never have been deterred from writing poetry if my Houston colleagues' judgment had not jibed with something already inside me, some insecure spot that made me feel that, on some level, I was an impostor. It had been a good long run, but it was time to stop pretending I was a poet.

# – On Not Reading Thomas Bernhard –

Some years ago I received a request from a friend, the deeply and widely cultivated Katharine Washburn, that I send her something for a literary journal she was coediting about Thomas Bernhard. Always eager to satisfy Katharine, in spite of my reservations on the subject, I eventually wrote the following in the form of a letter to her.

Dear K.:

When you asked me to contribute to your special number on Thomas Bernhard, I told you that I'd read only one book of his and had no plans to read more, and you replied with your irresistible voice of throaty mischief that that too could be the subject of an essay: *Why* did I not read Bernhard? At the time it seemed an amusing but far-fetched proposal, which I had no intention of accepting, since an honest answer to that question would have only exposed my intellectual limitations and unsupportable taste prejudices before an audience of unsympathetic Bernhardites. However, having just read Robert Craft's longish appreciation of Bernhard in *The New York Review of Books*, I was struck by the realization that, based on

Craft's summaries of the plays, novels, and memoirs in the Bernhard corpus, I was still not in the least tempted to read further. You ask me why this should be so. Well, for starters, the approving portrait Craft drew was of someone ferocious, solipsistic, bracingly intransigent, despising mediocrity and motherland – in other words, a self-important pain in the ass. Of course dedicated Bernhardites (one imagines them meeting in cellars around the Upper West Side) might well feel that the Craft article did not really do justice to their man, was shallow or typically *NYRB*-magisterial, missing the point, and that I ought not to be swayed by it. The point is that I wanted to be swayed by it, so as to steel myself for a lifelong neglect of this apparently important writer. If Craft is right that Bernhard will one day be studied in every American university, then I had better get some momentum going in refusing to read him further, before my courage collapses.

It wasn't always this way. I remember the first time I came across a fresh copy of Bernhard's novel *Correction*, around 1983, in the Rizzoli Bookstore (was it the original Rizzoli on Fifth Avenue, which I loved, with its Brazilian mahogany staircase and upstairs gallery and sexy monastic ambience, those premises since taken over by Henri Bendel's department store, or the second, present version on West Fifty-Seventh Street, which is more impersonal? – I think it was the old Rizzoli), on a table next to several other paperbacks from a new line, Aventura, the Vintage Library of Contemporary World

Literature. This display was almost pornographically tempting to me: first, because I am a sucker for book packaging that creates a snobbish, happy-few aura, and these trade paperbacks, featuring four-color painterly illustrations surrounded by lots of white, on thick white-card cover stock, and the bold calligraphic slash of an *A* for Aventura (the name itself conjuring one of my favorite movies) suggested the realized literary wet dream of a hotshot editor capriciously neglecting the bottom line; second, because my preferred reading consists of neglected foreign writers – I suppose I feel too competitive with my American contemporaries, but I am a comparative literature buff down to the toes, just give me an obscure book by a foreigner with worldly irony, something by Svevo, Pavese, Machado de Assis, Narayan, Pérez Galdós, Milosz, Bassani, Tanizaki, Soseki, Kundera (before he went popular), Eça de Queiroz, Canetti, Zoshchenko, and I'm in paradise. So I had every hope of adding Bernhard to my list of witty melancholics. The paperback carried a quote on the front from George Steiner, *Times Literary Supplement*: 'The feeling grows that Thomas Bernhard is now the most original, concentrated novelist writing in German.' 'The feeling grows': that gave me pause. Not Steiner's feeling but *the* feeling, the sentiment of educated readers everywhere. And where were you, Lopate, while this feeling was growing? Were you not, admit it, paying too much attention to the Mets, or going to movies, or reading only dead authors, okay, even dead German authors like Walter Benjamin and Robert Musil, but shamefully ignoring the living German writers, so that you were unable to offer a single rival of equally 'original, concentrated' merit to refute Steiner's claim? You thought you knew which way the wind was blowing, and yet all along a Bernhard monsoon was collecting offshore. Well, you had better get with it, my friend! On the other hand, George Steiner – do I really respect this man, or is he just some sort of pompous know-it-all? He writes serious, solemn book reviews in *The New Yorker*, which some people say are brilliant, but which always seemed to me no more than respectable – oh, respectable to the highest degree, mind you, it is probably only my stupidity that fails to grasp Steiner's unique contribution to modern thought. He did write that highly regarded essay on Russian literature, *The Hedgehog and the Fox* – no, wait a minute, that was by Isaiah Berlin, and Berlin really is brilliant . . . although, come to think of it, I've often finished one of Berlin's essays in *The New York Review of Books* and not understood what was so wonderful about it either. No, Steiner is the one who wrote that other little book about Russian literature, *Tolstoy or Dostoevsky*, which I read as an undergraduate and which left no impression on me. (Years after this Rizzoli episode, I went to a lecture by Steiner in the hope of settling the question once and for all, was he brilliant or not? His public manner seemed to me very impressive, erudite, definitely brilliant, though a day later I couldn't remember anything he'd said, except it was about a passage in Homer. Several feminist women friends of mine who were at that lecture told me later that Steiner was an old-fashioned male chauvinist who was trying to hide the fact in his public presentation, but I suppose it says something about my own untrustworthiness along these lines that I failed to pick up a hint of this tendency in him, just as earlier, when I read Bernhard's *Correction*, I didn't even notice that it was 'deeply marred by misogyny', as Craft puts it – or anyway, that wasn't what bothered me about the book.) I then turned the paperback over and saw 'Astonishingly original, a composition of strange new beauty' (Richard Gilman, *The Nation*). Wasn't Richard Gilman basically a theater critic who had married the powerful literary agent Lynn Nesbit? Was he trying to establish himself as more of a cultural heavyweight by trumpeting this dense, feverish (I had already peeked at the prose) Austrian writer, the way some movie critic will write a paean to an unassailable literary figure like Primo Levi, just to keep his intellectual stock up? On the other hand, maybe Gilman was already *there*, at the center of our intellectual life, and I had simply failed to realize this fact while spending too much time watching Mets games. Caught in a pincers movement between the combined authority of Steiner and Gilman, finding myself in a quandary of indecisiveness, I thought: oh, what the hell, it's not that expensive, and bought the book and left Rizzoli's. For a while it sat on my coffee table, impressing, I hoped, those visitors who might chance to examine the current pile. Then one afternoon, feeling rigorous and strangely clear-headed, I began reading *Correction*. Initially the fact that there were no paragraph breaks annoyed me, it meant that every time my eyes blinked I would lose my place, there were no chinks to provide footing on those solid cliffs of prose, I worried about eyestrain, plus the absence of visual caesurae made it harder for me to pace myself, to decide that a certain number of pages would constitute the day's quota, there were no chapter endings to aim for, so I kept reading, feeling vaguely migrainous, which I realized may have been the point, since the writing itself was so feverish, claustrophobic, resistant to characters or plot in the traditional sense, it was a sort of meditation, all well and good, I understood what he was doing, I wasn't born yesterday, it's not for nothing I read all those difficult books in my youth, Henry James's *The Golden Bowl*, all those hyperventilating narrators and tortured philosophers, Dostoevsky, Céline, Kierkegaard, Nietzsche, Handke, it was to prepare me for just such an experience as Bernhard, with his obsessively brooding tone, going around and around, bouncing like a metal bead in a pinball machine, wasn't this analytical stuff just the kind of thing I liked? Just my cup of tea? And yet, as I patiently plowed through the novel, twenty pages an hour at one clip, a little voice inside me was saying: This is hard going and is it really worth it? I pushed this thought aside, because I was eager to have a Bernhard under my belt, to have *done* Bernhard, enough to be able to brag that I'd gotten to him sooner than my friends. And indeed, when I finished the book I went around town telling everyone how brilliant it was, how they really ought to read it, *had* to read it, I was overstating my enthusiasm because after all I wanted some reward, some intellectual street credit for the effort I'd put in. I wanted to be part of that growing *feeling*, marching shoulder to shoulder with George Steiner and Richard Gilman and Susan Sontag and the rest, and even if none of them recognized me or acknowledged my greeting as we marched along, I knew, *I* knew that I had done my homework, I wasn't just a layabout watching the Mets game, I was someone who both watched the Mets *and* read Thomas Bernhard. I was a well-rounded individual, sound mind in sound body, *mens sana in corpore sano*, as we used to say back in Columbia College.

It so happens that whenever I discover a writer I like, I start acquiring all of his or her books, stockpiling them for that first summer day when I'm free from student papers and can read purely for pleasure. But I noticed that something seemed to be holding me back from acquiring other Bernhard titles. There was something a little too fanatical about him for my taste – too hothouse, too punitive, what have you. I wondered if he had a true sense of humor. What I missed in him that I enjoyed in my favorite ironists, from Montaigne to Machado de Assis, was that gyroscopic balance and self-skepticism, or modesty, which would rescue the analytical work from megalomania, so that even when the narrator seems self-delusional we can still catch the smiling sanity of the author underneath. I wasn't sure whether I could trust that Bernhard was truly detached from his ranting narrator. Maybe he was trying to show that detachment and objectivity were a myth, by bringing us into a claustrophobic space in which no distance, no perspective would be allowed – to rub our noses, so to speak, in the myopia and unhealthiness of self-absorption that he took to be the universal condition. If so, he had made his point, boy had he made it, like a dentist's drill, he deserved all sorts of credit for daring, experimentation, practicing on the cutting edge, a writer's writer, but it still seemed pretty much a trick, a tour de force, and I wanted – a novel. Better to praise him than to undergo the experiment again. If, as Craft informed us, '*Correction* is Bernhard's most profound work', I had all the more reason to keep away, since I had found his best not exactly to my taste.

My resistance to further burrowing in Bernhard was of a piece with a conscious effort to distance myself from what might be called 'the blackmail of the avant-garde'. Ever since I was a teenager, I'd swallowed the argument that I should experience a certain difficult artwork because it kept faith with the logic of modernism, so for decades I had paid my dues, digesting works whose stimulations barely compensated for their longueurs: I had waited patiently for the next theatrical image in a Robert Wilson opera to change onstage, listened to hours of Philip Glass's musical repeats, watched Michael Snow's mechanically programmed movie camera scan a barren landscape in 360-degree arcs, dutifully read Hans Haacke's polemical conceptual artworks about Manhattan real estate in art galleries, perused William S. Burroughs's cut-up poems in columns scissored from larger texts, all in the hope that I could convince myself that tedium was a necessary prelude to ecstasy. Now all at once it occurred to me that I had never signed a paper committing myself to the army corps of modernism. Nor did I regard myself as an antimodernist. It was simply that I could no longer be coerced into endorsing something because it claimed to be the next aesthetic step. If Bernhard extended Beckett, did that alone make him worth reading? Bernhard was a Jeremiah, the last angry, conscience-torn Austrian. Okay, let him have his fun, but I can't go along with a man who, for instance, makes such a big deal out of hating his country – not that one should necessarily love one's country, but why act so personally injured, so outraged, so *surprised* when it is run by mediocrities? Certainly Austria had much to answer for, having condoned anti-Semitism and Kurt Waldheim, but if indeed it is a ghost living on past grandeurs of the Austro-Hungarian empire, that should inspire pity, not odium. The narrator in Walker Percy's *The Moviegoer* may think 'Only the haters are alive', but Percy went on to disprove that by writing a lively novel about gentle human beings incapable of hate.

I'm not saying hate can't produce good literature. Céline, one of my favorite writers, makes an interesting comparison to Bernhard. Céline and Bernhard are both incessant chatterers, fanatics of a sort, unfair witnesses. So why do I tolerate fanaticism in the French writer, whose politics after all were completely reprehensible, unlike Bernhard, who was, if not a demo- crat, at least an anti-Fascist? It could just be that I stumbled on Céline in my adolescence, when his rage spoke to mine, but I rather think it's because he created vivid scenes and unforgettable characters in the great novelistic tradition, because he possessed a perverse comic genius filled with self-mockery and compassion that gave the lie to his self-proclaimed misanthropy, and because he engineered a cathartic release – that release that Bernhard for the most part puritanically refuses us. Of course I could be all wrong about Bernhard, having read only one of his books. But this letter is not meant to be a serious critique of Bernhard, only an analysis of my resistance to Bernhard. As such, it is also an analysis of my ignorance, for what else could you call the refusal to learn more about a subject? If it has any value, it is only to suggest how we retain calculated prejudices against this or that artist, so as not to be eaten up by the monstrous demands of high culture.

Another reason I have for neglecting Bernhard, which is also not the man's fault, has to do with the way that literary reputations are orchestrated in America – particularly the reputation of an estimable, difficult, supposedly underappreciated foreign writer. American readers are always being scolded by our cultural arbiters about how stupid and lazy we are, how we have no intellectual life compared to Europe, and how we can at least make a start in the right direction by consuming the intellectual flavor of the month. I feel conflicted in this regard, because I would give a lot to be one of those arbiters of cultural fashion, and I suspect that our intellectual life may indeed be small potatoes compared to Europe's (though how can I be sure, having never been a part of European intellectual life?), and I also agree that Habermas, Rulfo, Chiaromonte, et al. are worthwhile authors. On the other hand, I still freeze up at the thought that *they* may be trying to put one over on us, by exaggerating the merits of some of these foreign writers and soft-pedaling their flaws. For instance, I happen to be fond of the Swiss author Robert Walser, but I still can't accept his being packaged as a major writer when he is really an intriguing minor figure, on the order of Lautréamont, who may have inspired the Surrealists but was no Balzac or Baudelaire. Sometimes scholars become so hypnotized by the Lautréamonts and Walsers precisely because of their marginality, or because of their lopsided incompleteness, which allows for all sorts of speculation. Recently I was asked by an even more obscure journal than yours to contribute to their special issue on Robert Walser, for an equally invisible fee, and, being obliging, I turned in an enthusiastic commentary on *The Walk*. It *is* a beautiful story, but I didn't have the guts to state my deeper reservation, which is that, for all of Walser's eccentric charm, and he certainly deserves to be read – a barrel of laughs compared to Bernhard – I still can only take him in small doses before his precious, doll-like, arrested-development sensibility, whether faux-naïf or genuinely childish, gets on my nerves. He is, to put it bluntly, *cracked*, just as Bernhard seems to me, on some level, deranged. When I read either one, the obsessive language has a visionary intensity that can give exquisite insights into the limitations of normalcy. But it's also exhausting, the same way it is exhausting to listen to a paranoid schizophrenic for more than ten minutes. I have had some experience along these lines, a friend of mine had a mental breakdown that took the form of incessant panicked verbalization, logorrhea, the clinical term for which, I believe, is logomania. It was very distressing; it lasted for years; he would phone around eleven o'clock at night and talk in a rush for an hour until I had to hang up. In the end, he killed himself. Perhaps in saying this I have stumbled upon the key to my allergic reaction to Bernhard: I am made too nervous, too threatened by being put in proximity to that aggressive, suicidal, circular discourse, logic's noose, produced on the borders of sanity. That may be as close as I can get to an answer.

Sincerely,
P.

The above was written some time ago. My wonderful, husky-voiced friend Katharine died of lung cancer, after a lifelong smoking habit; Richard Gilman passed away as well, and any day I expect to read an obituary notice for George Steiner. In the meantime, I have read a second novel by Thomas Bernhard, *The Loser*, which struck me as magnificent, satisfying in every way, including character and plot, and an entertainingly haranguing, hilarious collection of essays, called *My Prizes*. I expect to go on reading this author with pleasure. Having expressed all my reservations about Bernhard, I am now free to like him. Go figure.

# – Coda: The Life of the Mind –

## 1

My writing office is on the third floor of a brownstone where my wife, daughter, and I have lived for the past fifteen years. When I look out the window in summertime I am aware of a generalized green from several old trees; in autumn the leaves turn auburn and fall off, and I can see much more clearly my neighbors' brownstones across the street. I've never put up curtains or window shades, and I am never sure how much my neighbors can see into my study, which is why I don't write at my desk in the nude (or not very often).

It is fortunate we are not yet living in an age when our thoughts can be mind-read; otherwise, my neighbors on the block would probably come after me with pitchforks. As it is, I have learned to offer a bland if brusque façade, which serves, just barely.

Our street, in Carroll Gardens, is a quiet one and used to be 90 percent Italian but now is more mixed-gentrified, with Chinese, Arabs, Jews, and whatnot: retirees, firemen, architects, shrinks, law professors, realtors, welfare clients, ex-criminals, art restorers, graphic designers, mentally ill outpatients, and, inevitably, several writers. I am glad the view from my window is fairly mundane and not breathtaking, as a vista too picturesque might distract me from writing. The old expression for cogitating is 'being in a brown study', and the muddy cocoa backdrop of brownstone façades and stoops across the way permits me to stay in my thoughts while I am dimly conscious of the lapping ambience of Brooklyn, the sounds of passing cars and the twittering of leaves. It is as though I am cocooned in a tree house. The muted colors outside my window are slightly blurred around the edges like a Corot painting (the more so because I am nearsighted and not wearing my glasses at the computer).

On the columnar spaces between the windows facing the street, and on every inch of the other three walls in my study, stand floor-to-ceiling bookshelves, and the spines of other authors' volumes, peripherally glimpsed, act as prods to keep me on task.

2

There is something about autumn that makes me want to rearrange my bookshelves: a soothing seasonal ritual, like carving pumpkins or burning piles of leaves. This fall, the impulse stole on me unexpectedly. I started to hunt for a book to read, when I noticed my Japanese literature section was overflowing, with excess paperbacks stacked horizontally above the tops of upright hardcovers, and others in danger of slipping behind the front ranks and disappearing from sight. The Italian section, I noticed, had a little extra room.

I could consolidate the two – but what connection did Japanese and Italian literature have, other than both countries having been Axis powers that fought against us in World War II? No, it would make more sense to move the Portuguese writers in with the Brazilians, and pair the Japanese shelves with the Chinese . . .

Before I knew it, I was cradling armfuls of books like a wobbly accordion. I tried to keep them in the same order, but whenever a book or two fell from my hands, the whole alphabetical system was endangered, and I would end up having to file every one separately, which was what I secretly wanted to do, because it gave me the chance to handle each volume, to finger the covers, to browse a bit in the pages. Not so much the books I loved as the ones I had neglected. At least one-third of my books I haven't gotten around to reading yet: I stockpile books for a rainy day, but if it were to rain continuously from now until I am ninety I might still not be able to finish every title. I have the unfortunate habit of going on book-buying binges and then forgetting what I have acquired. More than once I've picked up a classic (some Dickens, say, which I haven't read yet) in a used bookstore or stoop sale on one of my walks, only to discover that I already owned a copy at home.

These rearranging sessions serve to reacquaint me with my stock, and revive the desire to tackle previously daunting titles. I set these aside in a separate pile, an ambitious stack of miscellaneous items like

Wittgenstein's *Tractatus Logico-Philosophicus*, Nabokov's *Ada*, Pirenne's *Medieval Cities* – books which I approach with an expectation more to better myself than to receive pleasure. I place them carefully on the end table beside my writing desk, so that visitors may notice them and admire my intellectual rigor; in time, however, they become an invisible part of the furniture, and I return them to the bookcase regretfully unread.

But I am getting ahead of myself: back to the original organizing task. In a throwback to my childhood play with toy soldiers, I now control the movements of nations by dictatorially dispersing their literatures. Having rearranged the globe, hitched Spain to Greece and returned India to England, I am ready to tackle subtler diasporas. My books are distributed not only by nationality but by subject matter and genre, including categories such as movies, poetry, architecture, social science. Delicate decisions must be made. Once, to honor Freud's felicitous writing style, I paid him the compliment of putting him in German literature along with Rilke and Mann, rather than in the social sciences, where I had relegated such eminences as Max Weber. But then, I had never read much Max Weber, perhaps I was being unfair, so in the end I moved Freud back in with the psychologists and sociologists.

There are also certain sets, such as my complete Charles Lamb, that I want to feature, because I like their bindings, or their tallness requires a higher shelf, or their authors are favorites of mine. This caprice has wreaked havoc with the alphabetical system. At times I will take into consideration the writer's own feelings about whom he or she might wish to lie next to, and will match-make, placing Emily Dickinson at last beside Thomas Wentworth Higginson. In other instances I can be quite brutal about following a rigorous alphabetical schema, deriving sadistic sport at the thought of forcing antagonists in life or aesthetic manner to rub covers together.

The main principle of organization, I am embarrassed to admit, comes down to snobbery. I promote certain writers or national cultures that fascinate me at the moment, or that seem the gold standard of quality, while demoting others to the remoter shelves. Chilliest Siberia is a bookcase just outside my study in the hallway next to the bathroom, which holds those contemporaries of mine, rivals who have somehow managed to win wide public approval. Curious like everyone else, I had bought their books, read them with a mixture of disappointment and relief, and consigned them to the nether regions.

The beauty of my system is that nobody coming into my house and glancing at its library would suspect how sensitively the ordering reflects my discriminations. They would see a somewhat random assortment of books, whereas I perceive the fanaticism, pettiness, malice, and good taste of the person who has put the collection together.

3

One day I was idly going through new messages in my email when I came upon a request to contribute an essay to a volume, the proceeds of which were to go to the Save Darfur Coalition. The book's premise was that each contributor should expatiate on some risk he or she had faced as a writer. Reluctant as I am to write anything without being paid, and averse to boasting about my alleged nobility in overcoming fears, it nevertheless struck me that during my busy, preoccupied life I had neglected to save the people of Darfur. So I rolled up my sleeves and composed the following:

Every time I momentarily lose orientation, like asking myself in the midst of some domestic family squabble what am I doing here or who am I (such moments of vagueness do not decrease with aging), I think back to the last piece I wrote and tell myself, 'Aha, I am the author of ——.' It could be a lengthy tome, or a book review or a semihack article I wrote last week, doesn't matter, the point is that I experience an instantaneous congealing of self-confidence. Sometimes as I roam about on a break from writing I tell myself, like a parent reassuring a child, that I am the author of a whole shelf of books; it was always my dream to take up a shelf in the library, and I'm almost at that point, having written maybe a dozen titles, edited a half dozen more, and contributed ten more introductions to photography books or other authors' reissued texts that get my name put in however small type on the cover. You would think that anyone who had already generated so prolific a corpus (we will defer the question of quality for the moment, or indefinitely) would be mature enough not to have to resort to such petty incantations, but such is not the case. I need to pat myself on the back constantly, because without this reminder of my literary output I fear I would vaporize.

The negative corollary of this phenomenon is that every time I finish a book, I become quite morbid and think I am going to die soon. It is as though, having cleared the desk, I no longer have an excuse to live. Actually, even before finishing a book, when I am still in the final stages, I begin to have the hit-by-a-truck fantasy: walking through the streets of Brooklyn, I ask myself if my manuscript has reached a point sufficiently far along that, *were* I hit by a truck and killed instantly, it could still be published, with a short note, of course, by my widow or editor explaining the circumstances. I brood about where I left my manuscript, and if it is in an obvious enough place on my desk or the piles of papers beside the desk so that my wife could find it, after she has gone through the necessary grief-and-burial period, or so that she could locate it on my computer, and initiate the search for a publisher, assuming she liked it enough not to suppress it (one can never be sure about such things). Then the day comes when I have definitely finished the manuscript, for better or worse, and it is a book, or potential book. I take it to the photocopy shop and have three copies made. I give one to a friend and another to my agent. The third I leave with my wife. And I begin to think of death.

Sometimes these thoughts take the form of fantasizing approaching some friend, and asking him to become my literary executor. This fantasy of the chosen friend is shot though with Hawthorne-Melville unconsummated homoeroticism, except the brunt of this romanticized turn in the relationship will start from the moment I die, necrophiliacally, so to speak: Who will love me enough, once I become a ghost, to put up with the bother of being my executor? First I have to perform a rigorous analysis of all my friends and ask which one of them I trust the most. Many have let me down in the past; these are easily eliminated; but I must also cross off the list those dependable friends who are older than myself and who might not be around long enough to agitate to keep my books in print or, what is even more arduous a task, get the out-of-print ones reissued. There is also a large stack of my uncollected work (journalism, film criticism, book reviews, ephemeral poems, juvenilia), which a really alert, industrious literary trustee might find a way to see into print. How to locate all that material? To gather all my unpublished work together, the chosen literary executor would have to burrow into my files, a process that could easily take half a year. What matters is that, if the friend is successful, he will have added to my library shelf, which is all I care about.

The irony is that I have still not gotten around to composing a will, though my wife and my mother-in-law regularly nag me that it is my responsibility to do so. Writing a will is certainly practical, but this step would entail envisioning my extinction, and while I am happy to do so as an exercise in self-pity or an act of gothic imagination, I am less drawn to the idea of making life easier for those who will survive me. Let them suffer. Oh, I am sure in due course I will make out a will, but the prime motivation for it will be to settle this question of my literary executor.

When I finish a book I am dead, empty. It is at such junctures that I wish I had a knack for living. E. M. Cioran once wrote a book with the beautiful title *The Temptation to Exist*. I, too, have frequently been tempted to exist, but I am no good at it, and so I plod through the hours of leisure with a pretense of graceful participation which does not fool for a second those closest to me (my wife and daughter), and I wait impatiently for the next opportunity to sit at my desk and write. Anything. For it is only when writing that I begin to exist. In that sense I take no risks by writing: intensely honest self-exposures come easily to me, the most provocative positions that clash with conventional morality are a breeze, complex researches and ambitious structural challenges are finally child's play, next to the difficulty of getting through daily domestic life, trying to love one's family members on a consistent basis (despite the lack of respect they show me compared to the literary community), listening to the neighbors' small talk, and deciding which telephone company provides the best service package.

Notting Hill Editions is devoted to the best in essay writing. Our authors, living and dead, cover a broad range of non-fiction, but all display the virtues of brevity, soul and wit.

Our commitment to reinvigorating the essay as a literary form extends to our website, where we host the wonderful Essay Library, a home for the world's most important and enjoyable essays, including the facility to search, save your favourites and add your comments and suggestions.